THE
WOW
FACTOR

IN SALES

BUILDING
LIFELONG
RELATIONSHIPS

Written by **ANGEL MEDINA**

ISBN: 978-0-578-49527-9

*This book is dedicated to my beautiful wife, Lana.
She is there for me, believes in me, and always encourages me
to do more. When I told her that I wanted to write a book, her
response was: "What can I do to help?" Your love and
encouragement will never be forgotten. You are my "why."*

TABLE OF CONTENTS

INTRODUCTION

First off, I want to thank you for deciding to purchase this book!

It is my goal that when you are done reading or listening, you will be able to deliver what I call the "Wow Factor."

My name is Angel Medina, and I have been in sales for two decades, helping people qualify either to purchase or to refinance their existing home loan in order to either lower the payment, lower the rate, get funding for home improvement, or pay off unwanted debt.

I am one of the few in my industry who survived the recession. All of my friends I used to work with left the business for another career, as they felt like their business had dried up. As for me, I kept in touch with all my clients, even when there was nothing to give them—not to earn their business in the future but simply because my clients were like family and friends to me. They were people I simply enjoyed talking to. That is why I stayed in this career—because I knew that good people needed my help, and I liked helping good people and their families.

I love the way it feels when my clients say, "Thank you" or "We could not have done this if you hadn't come into our lives." To me it feels like how Michael Jordan must have felt when he would get the game-winning shot. But why is that? I think it's because I have always endeavored to be the best that I can be— for my family, my clients, and myself. I am passionate about self-improvement, which is a huge component of this book.

Typically, prior to working with me, my clients will tell me horror stories about how they were treated when working with other lenders. I learned that if I treated my clients with first-class service, like family, like a best friend, then naturally they would want to work with me. Not only that, but when I mastered the skills I learned in this book, it made my job quicker and easier.

The main reason I decided to write this book now is because we live in a society where there is always a new toy, gadget, or software that is supposed to save us time. However, the moment we take away human-to-human interaction, from whatever job we may do, the customers will fade away.

As technology has grown, a lot of consumers are feeling like they are just a number to the businesses they buy from. In their interactions with customer service, they feel like they are working with a robot rather than experiencing genuine human interaction. I love technology; however, I will never allow it to interfere with the relationships I have with my clients. Technology should be utilized to bring businesses and clients closer together, not estrange them.

Salespeople and businesses promise that technology will actually help them free up more of their time. And although this may be true in theory, most salespeople use it to *not engage* with their clients, relying on a machine to do the work for them. If these individuals continue to rely on technology as customer service, rather than a tool to get close to their clients, my prediction is that they will experience short-term success. I believe technology will ultimately hurt them when it comes to growing closer to their clients if not used correctly, and their businesses will suffer.

My book will help you prevent this from happening. You don't want to be at the water cooler blaming your failures on the economy. Long-term success comes from building real relationships, friendships with a real human-to-human experience.

We have all experienced bad customer service, and we all want to be treated in a way where we feel the professional we are working with wants the best of the best for us. If you have purchased this book, then that means already you are someone who wants to be the Michael Jordan of your profession, the Ritz Carlton and not the Holiday Inn.

The skills required to provide the "Wow Factor" to your clients—listening, utilizing technology effectively and thoughtfully, confidence, integrity, facing your fears, and dealing with negativity, just to name a few—are like a set of muscles you have to strengthen. And the bigger your goals, the harder you have to work.

My clients see me not just as another salesman but rather a household name. Many of my clients consider me as a friend or family member. This is what I want for you, reader. These types of relationships, in any business or profession, are what will bring you success, and, more than that, will make your job enjoyable.

This purpose of this book is not to teach you a new script or set of tricks, but the material will bring out a new skill set and a newfound greatness within you. Do you want to be really good at what you do? Or do you want to be considered *legendary* at anything and everything you do—whether it's being a father, friend, sister, brother, doctor, salesman, or barista? If the latter is true, give me your full attention. With a little work, you can surpass everything you ever imagined or dreamed you could be. With the right tools, the person inside you can become more; the person inside you can become a legend.

CHAPTER 1:

Getting Started

After going through the trenches with the economy crash in 2006 and reading and listening to hundreds if not thousands of books, I've learned that the one thing every great sales individual has in common is they love what they do and they truly want to help and lead their clients in the right direction. They all strive to give their clients—before, during, and after the sale—the "Wow Factor."

What is the "Wow Factor?"

The "Wow Factor" is simply a client feeling as if they are working with a true professional when they need it most. So, I hope after you either listen to or read this book, the one thing you can take away is how to make your clients feel confident about working with you—because you not only are there to guide them, but you also go that extra mile, and then you go the extra 10 miles.

Why? Not because you have to, but because you hold yourself to a higher standard. You provide 5-star service; you provide the "Wow" in your client's experience before, during, and after the entire sales process.

Harvesting

It's not a sprint. One of the things I always focus on is not how I can fill my pipeline but rather how I can help more good people. I ask myself questions such as: *Who can benefit from my services? How can I get in front of my clients in order help them, whether I work with them or not?*

A large percentage of salespeople always focus on the reward and not the harvesting. The harvesting allows them to not only grow more clients in the present but grow a lot more in the future for the right reason.

Do What Others Won't

So, how do you do you provide the "Wow Factor"? First, start by finding ways to call your past clients, just to say hello. Whether it's a holiday or their birthday, find a reason to keep in touch. Make videos on valuable information that will help them and share these with them personally. Add clients to your friends list on your social media accounts, like Facebook, and connect on LinkedIn.

Separate yourself from the rest of the pack by doing what others don't or won't. Don't fixate on doing everything perfectly; rather, take immediate action. While you're taking action, others will be complaining they don't have enough business.

I have studied successful people for the past 20-plus years, and what I have learned is that successful people do what others will not or are not willing to do.

Lifelong Learning

I am a big believer that what you don't know *can* and *will* hurt you, especially now, where anything you want to learn is at your fingertips. Whether you look it up online or find someone to personally teach you, there is no excuse not to learn more on a subject. I, like most, have learned a lot simply through trial and error; to me, it is better to fail than do nothing.

Successful people always want to learn what they do not know because they are curious, and they know it is vital in order for them to be the best they can be to provide their services. If they don't know, they will find out, so the next time, when approached with a similar situation, they will be not only prepared but an expert to the point they can teach others. Lifelong learning is a key to providing the "Wow Factor" and becoming the go-to person in your field.

I believe you need to always be a student of knowledge, and you are powerless if you do not acknowledge it. You want to become the type of professional you would want to work with. I also believe you need to be not only a student but a teacher. The more I teach, the more I learn. I have learned that teaching helps you remember the things you may have forgotten and makes you practice what you preach. Whenever I give my kids a lesson, I remind them that I am telling these lessons to myself, too, and I have to remember these lessons just like they do. Become a mentor and a teacher to others in your field.

Finding Your "Why"

What motivates me is my "_why_"; if you don't have your "why" established, then this is the reason you are where you are and not where you want to be. My "why" is my wife, kids, family, and friends, who I love and care about, and they motivate me to be the best I can be and more.

You need to think about your "why." If you don't know your "why," then it will be impossible for you to be motivated. Find your "why" by writing down what you want now and in the future. If the answer is money, you need to go deeper, as that will not motivate you in the long term, but what they money can do for you specifically will motivate you. What will you do with that money? How will it help the people you love in your life?

Like yourself, I always wanted more. I am literally doing everything I discuss in this book. I not only I talk about it; I live it. For me, I want an everlasting effect for anyone who reads this. I want you to have that moment where you say enough is enough, and you decide to stop lying to yourself, and you decide you want to be that person who is not going to let your upbringing or your past dictate who you become or who you will be.

Yes, being a good man means going to work and paying the bills, but is that all there is? Can you give something more back to the people you love?

If the answer is yes, and if you're ready to change how you give so that it represents the best in you, then I know this book will change your life for the better and ultimately change how you feel and act. The more you become who you were meant to be, the more you realize how much time you may have let slip away. What that does is motivates you even more.

So, whatever you do—whether you're in sales, a firefighter, an attorney, a teacher, or you own a construction or landscape company—just know that if you know you are not living up to your full capability, your full potential, then this will be your wake up call. Whatever you decide, you will look back and either be happy you answered it, or regret you decided to ignore it.

Chapter Assignment
- Write down three things you can do to get closer to your clients and bring more value to them.
- What can you do to become a teacher or mentor in your field?
- What is your "why"? What motivated you to read this book?

CHAPTER 2:

Hard Work + Determination + Dedication = Success

I look back at my life, and it makes me realize how some of my personality developed. I realized at an early age that if I wanted to be someone, I was going to have to learn as much as possible and work harder than the next guy.

Challenge Your Beliefs

I also realized my beliefs were not always mine. A couple sayings I heard quite often growing up were: "Money does not grow on trees" and "No good deed goes unpunished." Those are not my beliefs; they were said by my father.

You may have been led to believe many things as a kid, and I suggest you go back and think about all the things that were said to you and decide if these things are actually what you believe now or if those beliefs were decided for you.

Growing up, I was very interested in successful individuals and how they became successful in their fields. I was very into basketball, and there was a video about Michael Jordan, which really stuck with me. In the video, Michael Jordan said, "Motivation, plus hard work, equals success." It sounded too simple, but the truth is, we get older and we usually complicate that simple rule. I know I did for many years, as my younger days consisted of partying and working and not in that particular order.

No, I could say my surroundings made it tough for me, which now that I look back, it was only an excuse to blame on others rather than to point the finger at myself. My parents weren't always the most positive. My Dad would say things like, "Something good happened, so now I am just waiting for the shoe to drop."

He had his beliefs, but I decided at the age of 12 years old that his beliefs were his and I would replace any negative beliefs and turn them into a positive statement. For example, my Dad would say he hated Mondays, so I would say I love Mondays and, in fact, treat every day as if it were a Friday. I made sure to only focus on the bigger picture to help me get closer to my goals.

So, I replaced every negative belief I had, no matter what, silly or not, with a positive. For example, if I said I was not good at talking in front of a big crowd, I would stop and think about a replacement statement. I would say it over and over until I believed it, whether I was actually good at public speaking or not. You see, it doesn't matter if you bomb the first time; all that matters is that you move forward in facing your fear, as that is the only way any muscle will grow.

So, if you haven't already, go back to your memory bank as far back as you can and think about all the positive and negative things your parents taught you.

Take a moment and really think about it. Some people have had it worse, and some better, but it does not matter; all that matters is that you now have a choice to change that belief if it doesn't serve you.

You will find yourself possibly laughing a little, or maybe a lot. Some of the things you were told may have been things you would totally not agree with now, but you still may not be cognizant of it, which will not allow you to notice that your actions are being affected.

The Wow Factor

Shifting your thought patterns from negative to positive is not a do it once or twice type of action; it's a fall off the horse and jump back on it, make no excuses type of action. We will never be perfect, but you're allowed to aim for it.

My dad led me more with his actions than his words. The positive things I picked up from him are his ability to get up early every morning and work hard to provide for his loved ones as, it was his duty. Failure was not an option, nor was waiting for things to happen.

From my mom, I remember growing up learning I could sell her, or anyone, anything. She taught me never to be afraid of going after what you want; if you get a "no," just keep asking until you get a "yes." She would tell me, "Just ask, Son... The worst that can happen is you get a 'no.' "

We all must learn to keep what serves us and discard what doesn't when it comes to our beliefs.

Face Your Fears

Growing up, we all had natural abilities, and some more than others when it came to getting our way. Now the difference is what you did with the hand you were given. For me, I decided at a young age if I was scared of it, I would do it. So, sometimes it worked in my favor, and most of the time it did not.

At an early age, I would get it into fights with kids that I was scared of and always had to go out of my way to let everyone know I was not shy. As I got older, I had the self-awareness to recognize I had the ability to influence people around me, but it was up to me whether I used it for good or used that energy for bad. So, when I went to live with my Dad at the age of 11, I realized at that point it was a fresh start and that person was not me. From that point on, my thoughts and overall behavior changed in an instant.

My point is we all go through our fears as kids, and we either face our fears as kids, as adults, or both. Fear has whatever value you give it, and it's more important to have control when it comes to your fear than to be fearless. Fear is not always bad to have; to me, fear keeps me alert, as having no fear will get you into hot water. I choose not to let fear control me but rather use fear to be useful to help me get closer to my goals. After reading this book, you will be able to do the same.

Making Choices

All of you reading this have a story, and I am no different. I am the youngest of four kids, and my mom and dad divorced when I was four years old. From what I heard, I was affected the most from this, as I acted out in school and at home.

It did get so bad from getting into fights at school to getting suspended to the point I knew I was not headed on the right track at the age of 11, so I made a decision to live with my dad. Now I knew it would be no picnic, but I had no idea I was headed to boot camp. But I believe everything happens for a reason, and I felt living with him made me realize life doesn't hand you anything, no matter who you are or who you may think you are. You have to grab it or someone else will.

My dad and I were close, but I knew he would not let me do the things that I did with my Mom, such as getting into fights at school, getting bad grades, or hanging out with the wrong crowd. So, from the beginning, he had very strict rules, and from that point forward, in a split second, I made a decision to not get into any more fights and to do well in school.

The Wow Factor

Now, in case you're wondering about my name, that is simple. My Dad said he had a friend named Angel who he hung around with growing up. He said they were at club (not a gang) together, and let's just say "Angel was no Angel." But the story goes...that when Angel had to go to court, my Dad went with him for support.

Now Angel decided he did not want to wear the typical suit or even his best Sunday clothing. No, Angel decided to wear an outfit that made him feel comfortable as if he was in the park on a Sunday afternoon. Not surprising... But the judge did not like Angel strolling into court dressed inappropriately.

As they started, the judge said, "Look at you, coming into my court dressed in baggy pants, baggy shirt.... Look at you.... What do you have to say for yourself, ANGEL?"

You could hear a pin drop as the courtroom got very quiet. So, at that moment, Angel looked up at the judge and with a confident grin said, "Jealous?"

Now, my point isn't that you should talk back to a judge or even put yourself in that position to begin with. My point is, your actions are the result of what you have already decided to commit to. Good or bad, your results will blossom over time. You see, it takes work to fail or succeed. Yes, even to fail, it takes work.

You have to work at not doing the things you know you need to do. So, whether you're someone who, like myself, loves to play PS4 (I love playing FIFA Soccer) or watch Netflix, or maybe you enjoy getting drunk every night, your actions require work.

We all come from different upbringings. No matter what upbringing you came from, you are the person who decides what you want to believe at any point in order to commit to whatever it is you choose.

Chapter 2 Assignment

- Are there things you remember growing up that you heard from your loved ones that you did not agree with?
- Write down five sayings, such as, "Money doesn't grow on trees," and replace them with an affirmation, like, "Money comes to me easily and abundantly." Repeat this affirmation any time this negative thought reappears in your mind.

CHAPTER 3
Persistent not Insistent

As kids, we are always selling, and what I mean by that is when a kid wants something, they will ask more than once and will not give up until they get a yes or until they are taught otherwise by their parents to not continue to ask. When my kids would ask me for something over and over, I would not discourage them from asking; I would, however, tell them they have to give me reasons why I should say yes. This allowed them to continue to be persistent but to think more about what they wanted and why they wanted it and all the reasons I should allow them to have whatever it is they wanted at the time.

To me when a client tells me that I am very persistent, that is a compliment. With that being said, a lot of times when people in sales are trying to earn someone's business instead of being persistent, they mistakenly are insistent.

The definition of insistent in the Merriam-Webster Dictionary is "existing for a long or longer than usual time or continuously." However, the definition of persistent is "continuing firmly or abstinently in a course of action in spite of difficulty of opposition."

So, when you're trying to win over the love of your life, you would never demand them to want to be with you or even to want to love you. However, it is a good thing to be persistent, as being told, "No, I do not want to go on a date with you," does not always mean they don't want to go on a date with you. For example, when I met my beautiful wife, I was told "no" several times. She will say it was only two times, but it felt like 10 times!

Angel Medina

To me, being told the word "NO" at the time simply meant I had to keep asking and finding alternative things and interests we had together to eventually have her say yes. I was fully committed, as I knew, given the chance, she would know I was sincere, and I only spoke from the heart.

Commitment

It's easy to say never give up, but if you keep doing the same thing over and over and you get no results, then giving up will be on your mind. I believe you have to have qualities that you either learn through life's lessons the easy or the hard way. Not only should you never give up, but never stop learning and always do the right thing. Deep down, we all know what that is.

I am sure there are many times you will look back on your life and you will remember a time that you felt defeated, but you didn't give up and you ultimately got what you wanted. So, the reason I am telling you to be persistent is not so you can always get your way, but in order to provide what I call the "Wow Factor" to your clients, you have to be undeniably committed.

I had a client who had a hard time due to her schedule, like most people do, so I knew I would have to do more by helping this client any way possible. So rather than rely on the client to get me what I needed, I asked her to rely on me to get her tax returns by speaking with the CPA, her insurance by calling her insurance agent, etc. No questions asked. I was willing to do anything I could to.

Most of the other lenders she came across said, "Here is what I need. Please send it, and when I get it, I will continue to help you." But if they had taken the time to hear this client's aches and pains, they would realize that this client was an RN who worked nights and slept during the day. She had very limited time off during business hours.

So, do more not to get paid more but to provide what others will not. You do not always get paid for doing things, but you do them because you know it's the right thing to do. There are many things we do right now that require a lot of our time and attention that we do not get paid for, but we do them because we know it's the right thing to do.

By you being committed to your clients and always doing more than what your clients expect or even what your company expects from you, you are gaining more than a commission check; you are gaining a new relationship. With that in mind, by you not focusing on the fruit but focusing on the root, you are building a stronger foundation for your future.

An example of going the extra mile will ultimately depend what your career field is. If you're a doctor, and you prescribe medicine to your patients, and you reach out to them constantly to make sure the prescription is working for them, you are in turn doing more than what your patients expect.

Now, how many of us can say that our doctor calls us after they prescribe a prescription to ask us how the medicine is working? Not very many. That is what motivated me to write this book, in hopes to bring back customer services and in order to make companies realize that their actions are destructive. Companies that neglect customer service will soon realize you can never replace a human being to sell their product. Companies must focus not only on getting new customers but also that they make sure to exceed the expectations the clients they acquire. The simple fact is, most companies are average and treat customers like a revolving door—in and out. It's a bad method to have. When one person reaches out to another and is committed to helping, that's customer service in action.

Chapter Assignment

- Write down three things you are doing for your clients that separates you from everyone else. *Example: I have all my clients make a personal video answering the question: "What was your experience like working with Angel Medina?" This gives them the opportunity to give me feedback and also provides me with valuable testimonials.*

CHAPTER 4:

Integrating Technology With Your Service

Gauging Your Clients' Technological Abilities

Sometimes, with how much we rely on modern technology, we forget that not everyone finds it useful in their day-to-day lives. I have learned never to assume that somebody is particularly tech savvy. A lot of salespeople not only expect their clients to be tech savvy but also get frustrated when they are not.

If you approach every client in the beginning as if they were your grandparents or someone you know who does not like technology, you would treat every client differently from the offset. So, for me, when I have a new client, I always start off with the assumption that they are not computer savvy and make sure to be alert by asking the right questions.

By asking the right questions, you will then learn whether or not your client is comfortable with technology. The ability to ask the right questions is your most valuable tool you have as a salesperson. You don't want to ask Mr. Smith, "Are you good with technology"? Just like you wouldn't ask someone you really like if they like you or not upon first meeting them.

For example, asking a client if they are near a computer may sound like a simple question, and it is, but the key here is to be alert and listen to not only what they say but *how* they say it—this part isn't as simple. This example could be relevant to any field you are in. With the majority of professions out there, more and more, whether we like it or not, technology is a force to be reckoned with.

Ultimately, you want to make a series of questions that categorize your clients on what technical ability they have so you can make their life easier and make working with them simpler.

Using Technology in Your Profession

In this day and age, if you are not on social media sites because you don't care to partake, nor do you want to deal with any of the "social media drama," but your business relies on referrals from clients, family, and friends, then you are, in a nutshell, shooting yourself in the foot. Even famous professional athletes or movie stars know that they must be on certain platforms in order to get more exposure and maintain their success.

A lot of people who don't keep up with the social media trends in their field simply do not feel it will make them money right away. But I hope you know after reading this book that just because you do not get paid to do something does not mean it will not be a waste of your time.

You must be a household name and continue to be on people's minds by focusing on doing what you can do to get closer to your goals—even if you may not want to do it. Use technology for its intended purpose, which is to help yourself get closer to your clients, streamline the process for them, and let them know that you are a 5-star professional.

Also, remember, technology can either be our friend or our worst enemy. It could either grow your business or make you feel as if we are running on quicksand. Use technology thoughtfully when it comes to helping your clients and promoting yourself.

Chapter Assignment
- Think about a time when technology has caused problems between you and a client.

The Wow Factor

- Write down a technology you are using today and how it helps you to become more valuable to your clients.

CHAPTER 5:

The Art of Listening

A lot of people in sales say something in such a way to get a reaction before they decide to explain it. When I am going over anything, the goal for me is not necessarily to get a reaction but rather to communicate authentically so that a client knows that I am not there to tell them what they want to hear but rather tell them what they need to hear.

In order for my clients to accomplish their goals, and in order for me to help them do that, I have to look within myself so that I may give them my advice, opinion, and guidance to the fullest extent. In speaking this way, they know for a fact what I'm saying is only for their benefit and is 100 percent truthful.

In order for me to speak from my heart, I have to first find out what exactly their goal is, not only now but in the future. In order to do that, you must learn the art of listening.

Now that is something that is easy to say but very hard to do. You need to not only listen to *what they are saying* but go beyond by focusing on *how they say it.* A lot of people are in their heads, not truly listening but rather thinking of the next thing they are going to say.

What I suggest in the beginning, and it's just like with anything, is to build that muscle. In order to build your listening muscle, you must first practice the basic fundamentals of listening. So, what I would suggest is when you are listening to somebody, truly listen and don't say anything to the point where they ask you "Are you listening?" before you have a response. By doing this, you are not waiting for your turn to speak but rather waiting for them to finish. So, if you ever find yourself listening to somebody and you have that itch to say how you feel, that is not listening.

Now, the next step would be to focus on how they are saying it. If someone says they really want to lower their payment and also get an overall lower rate but emphasize the word "payment," you will pick up that the rate is not the issue nor their concern.

Now, with that being said, it's not exactly just the "payment" that is their pain. In order to find out their pain, you must find their "why." So, you know to listen, when you hear what they have to say, then keep asking, "Why?" The "why" is the shell to the hardboiled egg. In order to crack that egg, each hit is asking the right questions to get their "why."

What I mean by pain is what pain that payment is bringing. Additionally, you must discover what type of pleasure would they get by lowering their payment.

In order to find out what that pain is so you can come up with a solution, you have to listen and not only listen but focus on what they are emphasizing and what is important to them. Separate what is not important to them so you can fine tune what they truly want. The better questions you ask, the more trust you gain. More trust equals honest answers, and honest answers will allow you to help your clients and their family, friends, and anyone they speak to.

In everyday life, a lot of people say that they are not good at selling or they are not good with working with people. But in everyday life, you are constantly selling, whether it's you selling your kids to do good in school or you are selling your spouse why they should go to the movies with you.

Here's an example. If my wife tells me that she wants to get a dog, and I just say, "I don't think that's a good idea," she may interpret that in different ways, depending on how well she is listening. If she heard me say "think" in a soft, low tone, she will first validate my opinion by agreeing, then ask, "Why?"

Through the words I say and how I say them, she will determine it's not the dog I do not want; it's the pain the dog will bring if it is not taken care of.

So, by her listening to the reason why I don't want a dog and knowing that it's not the dog itself but the possible pain that the dog can bring to our family, she would agree with what I am saying at that moment. By agreeing with me, she is then essentially opening up my mind, causing me to think about it more, which in turn will allow me to be more open to the idea of getting a dog. If she simply tries to get her point across, I will be put on the defensive, thinking of more reasons I don't want a dog.

By validating my response and my why, it allows me to in return not only speak how I feel but listen to what she is saying, and that way I can in turn find out how she feels about the pleasure of getting a dog. Now, by her responding, "I agree," what that does is it tells me that she is listening to me, but it then opens up the floodgates of what she has to say.

If she were to respond to me by acknowledging by shaking her head with agreement for example as if to yes I agree with her body language then it let me know she is truly listening and not waiting for her turn to talk but truly listening and interested as to hearing how I feel. That would make me happy and feel good because she's not only listening; she's going *beyond* listening. Now listening is one part of it. Going beyond listening means you *truly* are understanding what they are saying by their tone fluctuation, how they emphasize certain words, or even if you hear any grunts or deep breaths, and this is going to then ultimately get you what you want. You are truly discovering how that person feels.

By listening to how that person feels, you may realize that what they are feeling is not actually true. What I mean by that is if I am saying I do not want a dog, but I emphasize the words "DO NOT," I may sound like I'm saying that I do not feel we will properly watch the dog or give the dog enough attention.

By responding to me that the dog will be in a *loving home* and we can give *attention* to that dog so it will *feel loved* and to have a *good life* rather than being in a dog pound, that will ultimately do something inside of my mind and cause me to think about all the things that will be pleasurable about getting a dog.

It will also cause me to think about all of the reasons why *not* getting a dog will be painful. The things that may be painful are thinking of the dog in a *dog pound* and how that dog will be *put to sleep* if a loving family does not adopt that dog.

You see, my wife is really good at selling me on things, but she tells me all the time that she is not good at selling anybody on anything and is not good with people. That's the great thing: she does not know that she is good at it, so in turn it comes across like she is not trying to sell me, but she is truly doing what comes to her naturally.

You see, the truth is that we are all naturally good at listening and good at knowing right from wrong. What happens is as we get older, and we communicate with more people, and we get influenced by things around us, it conditions us to believe that by proving out point we will ultimately get what we want, not by listening.

The fact is, we all know right from wrong, and if you think about it, knowing right from wrong will then tell you what the right thing to do is. Next time you communicate with someone, ask yourself: *Should I truly listen to what this person is saying by putting myself in their shoes, or should I wait for my turn to talk so I can prove my point?*

Accepting Fault

Another thing I try to keep in mind while listening is if I say something wrong. If I am wrong, I want to be the first one to point it out and validate their point. Not only does this let them know that I am listening to what they are saying, but the person I am speaking with can also learn how to be a better listener. I do not feel there is ever a point to where you can say you are perfect; however, I feel you can strive to be perfect in different areas of your life. So, when your striving to be a perfect listener, your subconscious mind will then always strive to be more alert when others are speaking to you.

Practice Listening

The next time a client or anyone your talking with tells you something, truly listen and don't say anything to the point where they ask you, "Are you listening?" When that happens, you want to let them know you are listening, but you want to be sure they are finished and ask if there is anything else that is important for them to express. You want to continue doing that, and what that is doing is working out your listening muscle. It's like anything else—the more you work it out, the better it will get.

Even if you have been in the sales business for a long time and you're successful, you're not excluded here. This is a muscle that everyone should be strengthening. In fact, if anything, by being in the business you're in, whether you're selling Avon or insurance, you want to always improve your listening skills and anything else that can help you bring value to your clients. So, listening is a piece of the puzzle, and if you do not have that piece, you're not living to your potential.

Chapter Assignment
- Write down how you feel you can improve how you listen to others more effectively.

CHAPTER 6:

Keeping Customer Service Alive

If you are in the business of selling, it is your obligation—it is your duty—to keep customer service alive. What I mean by that is you want to make sure that you're doing everything to provide the best experience, the best service, to your clients and you are leading by example. I don't mean that you have to kiss your client's butt or laugh at all of their jokes; I mean that you should provide a genuine, friendly, honest experience.

By keeping customer service alive, I also mean that you must give back by recognizing those individuals who are providing you a white glove service. Do everything you can to promote them. If you go to someone and purchase a product, and someone provides you with what you think is above-average customer service, go out of your way to let their manager know how great they are doing. Write a review about them online, brag to your friends, and refer them. If you do this, you are then essentially keeping customer service alive.

I'm sure a lot of you out there are seeing a trend of places going out of business but seeing other places rise to the top by providing not the greatest product but what could be considered the best customer service. Now your definition of customer service may be different than your folks' or your elders', and why shouldn't it be? Everything has changed with technology, down to the way you purchase a new product. A lot has changed, but the fact is, a lot has stayed the same. So, to me, customer service is when you purchase a product or pay for a service, and when you are provided that product or service, you feel as if that person exceeded your expectations and *wowed* you.

For example, let's say that you go and purchase a pair of shoes and you tell that salesperson that that you're looking for shoes to go to a wedding.

That person then asks you, "What size shoe do you wear, and what color were looking for?"

You then respond, "I am a size 8 and looking for red shoes to match my red dress."

Now, most salespeople would say "Okay!" and then go and get you what you want, but let's look at a different way of handling this interaction. The salesperson instead replies, "Perfect! Is there anything else that is important to you?"

You might respond, "Actually, there is. I have a wide foot...so can you please bring me shoes that can accommodate my feet?"

The salesperson then says, "Of course! I am so glad that you asked, and I want to make sure I provide you with exactly what you are looking for. Before I go back to get the shoes, I want to make sure, is there anything else that is important to you?"

You respond, "No that is it."

Now, the average salesperson would stop at "Okay!" and bring back the shoes. They may be getting the customer what they asked for and meeting their expectations, but they are not exceeding them.

Let's return back to the salesperson who is going above and beyond. This person not only goes back to get the red shoes in a size 8 with additional width but also has another store member ask you if you would like something to drink while you are waiting.

This salesperson comes back and brings you, say, three or four different pairs of shoes to try on. Not only does the salesperson bring back multiple options; she also makes a recommendation for a shoe style based on the style that she detects you would like when she considers your clothes, the shoes you are currently wearing, and your handbag. Since this salesperson is in the business of selling shoes, she prides herself on being up-to-date and knowledgeable about fashion.

After she brings the shoes and gives you a recommendation, she asks you, "What color are the bridesmaid dresses, and what season is the wedding in?"

You tell her, "They are all wearing purple, and it's this spring."

She says, "Great! Now being in the industry that I am in, I would like to recommend a lighter, more neutral color, so I brought out a pair of beige shoes for you to try on as well."

Now, at that point, you try on the pairs of shoes. Since you can detect that this salesperson is "in the know" when it comes to fashion, you ask her for her opinion as to what color she would recommend for a dress. She tells you that although red is a great color and she knows that you already have a red dress, you should consider checking out some other dresses at a nearby store so that you can get a second look. She recommends a lighter pastel color for a spring wedding.

Now, customers and clients may take your advice, or they may not, but what you are doing if you follow this salesperson's lead is providing them your expertise and proving your knowledge.

Now, let's say you take her up on that offer and buy the beige shoes. She also lets you know that before you go to the store she recommended, she will let the sales rep know you are coming and will have him bring out several dresses for you to try on that will go with the beige shoes.

Most salespeople would stop at the sale of the beige shoes, but this salesperson is providing the "Wow Factor." She not only lets the sales rep at the other store know that you are coming but also lets him know to provide you with excellent customer service and asks him to call her when you show up at the store.

When you show up, the sales rep at the dress store calls the shoe salesperson, who asks to speak with you. She says, "Hey, I just wanted to say hello and to let you know that my friend who is helping you is going to provide you with excellent service, and not only that, I told him to make sure to give you 50% off of any dress that you choose. Also, if you feel you do not find what you are looking for, I want you to know that you can return the shoes anytime hassle free."

She further tells you that she can send you pictures of other shoes that she feels you may like, just in case you want more options. Essentially, what she is doing is going out of her way to do more, and yes, providing you with way more than you want.

Now you may get a lot of people who don't want that service and don't want your opinion, and that's fine, but what you are doing by going that extra step and then jumping onto the next three steps is guaranteeing that not only will that person not forget you; they will recommend you to anyone they speak with.

So, what I just described is just one example of what you can do in a particular industry, and this applies to everything across the board. You want to bring your customers a higher standard, a higher value, something more than what the average zombie sales reps provide. I say the word "zombie" because that essentially is what most people experience when shopping or looking to hire a person to provide a service. Most people consider themselves just employees, thinking they are simply there at work because they have to be, not because they want to be.

The Wow Factor

I say, if you're going to be somewhere, then *be there*! Whether you're a janitor, cook, or a cashier at a fast food place, take pride in whatever you do, as that is living.

The example I just gave you is extreme, yes, and may seem overbearing or intrusive. Most people don't want to come off as too aggressive. But do you want to be average? If you're reading this book, then I know you don't. So, my point is, by you giving your customers more than they ask for, and I don't mean by just giving them more just for the sake of it but really giving them more, you will bring more value to the interaction.

In whatever job you're in, you should be not only providing a service; you should be making sure to stay on top of the local trends; you should be constantly sharpening your sword by staying "in the know" with your profession. Now, that may mean that you have to do a lot of things in your off time that you don't get paid for, but if you focus on learning a new skill that will allow you to offer more value to your clients, you will be closer to providing that "Wow Factor," which will ultimately separate you and make you the dominating force in your field. Why not do things in your off time to do *the right thing*, which is do whatever is necessary to educate yourself so that you can provide the best service to anyone that you come into contact with? You have to ask yourself: if you were to have someone help you, would you want average service, or would you rather feel as if you just experienced greatness?

Chapter Assignment

- Describe the perfect sales rep. How would they act? How would they dress? How would they would provide value to their clients? You want to strive to do everything that you can in order to be that person so you can provide the "Wow Factor."

CHAPTER 7:

Professional Versus Sales Rep

We have all had that experience where someone has helped you and you felt as if you were at a 5-star resort. You looked at this person and you thought to yourself, *What makes this person love their job so much?* You can't help but feel as if this person has a unique quality or gift; you knew you were experiencing quality customer service and, more to the point, you wanted to write a review for this person. Why? Because they deserved it! In fact, you wondered why this person did not own their own company.

Here's an example. My office is in Downtown San Diego, and I was going to get my chicken sandwich, and I will be honest, I am picky with my food regardless of where I go, and I am not shy when it comes to ordering what I want and having it exactly how I want it.

Now, I go into the sandwich shop and order my sandwich just the way I like it. I would go back to this particular location because when I walked in, there was an employee that would greet me by name and would say, "The usual?"

I would smile and nod.

Not only that; he had a great attitude. Now does this person get more money for doing that? No. Is he it for tips? No. What he gets is much, much more, as I'm he sure gets satisfaction in knowing he is striving to live up to his full potential.

Now, it's impossible to always live up to your potential, but you can get close, and a small percentage of people do. You don't want to do only as you are asked in order to live, day by day, do you? It sounds boring, right? That's because it is; living that way is not normal, but most people will say it is. I live every day knowing that everything I do today will impact me in the future. So, to me, every day is an opportunity for me to improve myself in order to be the best person I can be. It is my obligation to be the best person I can be in order to provide for my loved ones while leaving my footprints.

We all have a choice in everything we do, and by going that extra mile and not doing it for something in return, you are moving towards living up to your full potential, which means much more than monetary compensation.

Being a professional is doing more than what is asked of you and more of what you ask from yourself. We all have come across this person, whether it was a mechanic, dentist, doctor, or lawyer. You will notice the professionals have this glow, as they have a higher purpose in life. To me that is living, and to me, not living up to my potential takes just as much effort.

You see, whatever you decide to do, if you're going to do it, make a choice to do it with pride. Do it whether you are getting a million dollars or doing it for free. Make your actions represent you. That is a professional, someone who works as though they are on the receiving end of their service, regardless of compensation or recognition. They are treating the customer exactly how they would want to be treated if not better because they know what it's like to be on the opposite side.

You see, I am also sure you are aware of the other side of the coin, which is experiencing horrible customer service to the point you wondered why this person even showed up to work or why they are even working at their establishment at all. Everyone at one time or another experienced horrible customer service and, if anything, could not wait to complain about this individual.

The Wow Factor

When I work with my clients, I tell them if there is something I can do to make the experience easier, faster, or better, it will be done for them. I am not nice in the beginning, when meeting with a client, and at the end, when closing out a contract, offering a fake smile and telling them I hope to work with them again; telling them I hoped they enjoyed my service; and telling them I hope they will refer me to their family and friends.

There is no hoping. I am not hoping, I am knowing. Why? Because I provided stellar professional customer service and on top of that did more that what they or my company expected me to do.

It's not for the reward because if you're doing it for that, it will show; rather, when I am providing a service, I know everything I do is a reflection of me. I want to provide spectacular customer service to the point they never want to work with anyone else again but me, and not only that, they only want their family and friends using my services because they know that I am providing first-class customer service and much, much more. Not because I have to but because that is just who I am, and they know that I do it for the love of what I do, and I do it with a higher purpose.

Now they may not know what that higher purpose is, but they know it's well-intentioned and they know whatever it is it makes me highly effective and highly attentive to their needs

But, again, it is a constant choice, as I am not perfect; even writing this book, I feel there are a lot of things that I am working on in order to accomplish my goals, as I feel I am not close to where I want to be, and that is not a bad thing. I also look back to see how far I have come. I use my past success for motivation.

Angel Medina

There is always a beginning. All the great people out there who have gotten to where you want to be have had to start from humble beginnings. You have to just do something.

One way to do something more for your clients is always asking yourself, *What I can do to make my process easier and more pleasant for them?* When you come up with the answer, don't rationalize it, think about it, or come up with 10 different ways to make that happen. Just do it. Don't overanalyze it. When you act and move forward, things happen.

Growing up, my dad would call me "the man with a million excuses." Now, I did not like this because to me it meant I was lying to him, but the reality was that it was true. Mainly I was lying to myself, and he was calling me out on my lies. Because this bothered me so much, I knew that making excuses was just a reason I made up to not do what I needed to do. My dad may have not said gently, but I felt it did teach me that excuses were not a good thing at all, and it caused me to change my behaviors and start taking more action instead of coming up with reasons not to do the things I needed to do. Don't make excuses and start doing more today.

Chapter Assignment
- Write down the reasons why a client should choose you over your competition.

CHAPTER 8:

Welcome the Haters

When you start providing more than is socially expected, haters' ears will perk up. As a result of doing more, your results will start to blossom. Knowing that, understand that there will be haters who will make comments that sound like brotherly advice. The reason being: you are doing what the haters know they should be doing but choose not to because they have managed to come up with every excuse in the book.

The truth is most successful people or individuals who want more out of life typically do not have time to hate on other people; if anything, when they see someone doing more, they feed off of their energy and they always wish this person nothing but success. Haters are not successful people and are envious of your hard work.

Having haters is a sign you are on the right path, and you need to welcome them instead of letting them you bring you down or take away your mojo. And the more prepared you are, meaning the more you're working on your A game on a daily basis, tirelessly, the more confident you will be.

Responding to a Hater
Every successful person will tell you that they were criticized by others for doing the things they did to attain success. Even right now, as I am writing this book, I get discouraging comments like, "How are you going to have time to do that with you already working so much?" or "You do so much. How do you have time to spend with your family?"

When I hear things that are anything than positive, I always respond, "Thank you for your advice, but I only want positive feedback or encouragement." That stops a hater dead in his tracks and prevents further negativity.

You May Be a Hater

In turn, the people I surround myself with know that I will always be positive to them, as well, with whatever their dreams are. I will always say, "Yes, I know you will make it happen," because I love to see people go after their dreams.

You may very well be a hater or maybe you were a hater to someone in your life. If this is the case, I encourage you to recognize this and start wishing success onto others. Discouraging others won't make you successful by comparison. Everyone makes mistakes, and everyone can feel envious at times; what is important is that you recognize if you have tried to bring someone down and change the way you respond to people. This comes from strengthening your own positivity. As I mentioned in Chapter 2, any time you feel a negative thought creeping in, replace it with a positive one.

Haters May Be Closer Than You Think

Haters won't wear a sign saying, "I am a hater." You may even get people around you, such as your family, friends, or even people you work with telling you things like, "You can't have it all" or "You're doing great. You don't need to work so much." Be cognizant of this and know that these people say things like this because they are envious or have given up on their dreams. They're feeling hopeless.

Don't ignore it, don't deny it, but rather, just be alert. Don't let haters' words cause you to question your actions.

The Wow Factor

Steel Yourself

If you want to be more than average, then you will have to be prepared for people around you who will criticize you for their reasons, but see it as a compliment, knowing you are on the right track. Most people only do what society considers the normal, but because if you refuse to be average and commit to living up to your potential, though you will first get criticism, eventually these same people will end up admiring you. So do not dwell on it and or use any of your valuable time being upset.

When I would start at a new company, I would ask who the top guys were and try to get to know them. As for everyone else, I would be very polite but not spend that much time with because my time was very limited. My goal was always to be the top person in any company that I worked in, and I was not shy about letting others know that this was what I wanted and what was going to happen.

When you do this, others will start to do what you do. If you stay late, they stay late. If you make 50 calls, they try and make 60 calls. But when that would happen, I would not be a hater; I would be congratulator.

Unfortunately, it was pretty common to see these people have a good start and a good run but lack stamina. And as they would start to get tired while I was still pushing...that's when the hating began.

I once had an individual who started to stay come early and stay late, as that is what I would do to make sure to always get a good start and I would not stop even when I was the top sales rep or I was getting very close. One night, this individual asked me what company I came from, and once I told him, he then started to tell me all the reasons he was going to destroy me in the months to come. Well, at that point, I simply asked him how much he closed the month before. He told me with a grin, knowing it wasn't great, but he felt his pipeline was so full I would not stand a chance.

I congratulated his pipeline and said although he had a lot and he was looking to have a great month, what he was projecting to close I had already funded for the month. So, even if I did nothing, he could still not destroy me.

Did I let this hater's attitude bother me? No. It made me more confident! Anyone who makes negative comments or criticizes is really telling you that you're going above and beyond, and they're not doing what they should be doing.

So, in the beginning, it may hurt your feelings when you start to improve yourself and haters begin to notice, especially if it comes from a good friend or family member, but it's like anything else, the more it happens and the more you overcome it, the stronger you will become. Every success will build more confidence.

Chapter Assignment

- What does it mean when someone is saying something negative about you?
- Write down why having haters is not a bad thing and how you can use it in a positive way.

CHAPTER 9:

Bring Your A Game

If you are not disciplined with life, then life will discipline you. Yes, it's that simple. Often, we know what we need to do, but we make the decision to either do it or not. If you are drinking, doing drugs, or depriving yourself of sleep, you will not bring your "A" game. You will not have the "Wow Factor," no matter how good you are. You may do well in the short term, but not the long run. I have read hundreds of books on sales and successful people, and one of the things these authors talk about consistently is *health*.

Without good health—meaning getting proper sleep, not partying, and eating foods that will provide your body with energy and nutrition—it is impossible to be the best you. Speaking from personal experience, I already knew all of this but chose to ignore it for a long time.

Success is important, and keeping it is more important. Being on you're A game is how you're going to keep your success. And being on your A game is more than just how you take care of yourself physically; it also comes down to your mindset and how you relate to the world around you.

I used to subconsciously blame others for my challenges. This all changed one day when a mentor said to me, "People will do things you don't lie or don't agree with, but if you react in a way where you fire back or act worse than they did, you are just as bad." Never let anyone take you to their level; always stay in control and be the person you know you are, which is someone who has integrity, high morals, and class. What my mentor said to me stuck with me big time. I sat there thinking about it and realized he was right. And from that point forward, when someone was rude or disrespectful or something bad happened to me, I made sure to keep my composure and react in a way that I would expect my own children to react—finding the positive, focusing on the solution, and always keeping their composure.

One of the biggest reasons I feel this chapter is so significant is because if you don't do certain things, such as working out, trying to eat healthy, getting enough rest, staying away from drugs and alcohol, and cultivating a positive mindset, you can never be transforming your energy; therefore, you can't bring out the best in yourself. For example, if you see someone like Michael Jordan, all you're seeing and all everyone else is seeing is his success, but we have no idea of everything he did outside of winning championships; we only see his wins. So, what you do when no one is looking is just as important, if not more important, than what you do when they are looking when it comes to living up to your potential.

I recently read an online article in *The Huffington Post* by Dr Ali Binazir, and he declared that the odds of being born is about 1 in 400 trillion. That blew my mind and made me realize that every person on planet earth has a lot to contribute. I also realized that I needed to be sure to live up to my full potential by taking more action and doing more. Everyone who is born, no matter what, has something to give back to the world because our very existence is miraculous. We need to look in the mirror and ask ourselves every day if we are living up to our potential.

I want you to know that I ask myself that question every day. Not only do I ask myself that, I have to answer honestly to myself. You can lie to others, and quite frankly, you can lie to yourself. Asking yourself every day, "Am I living up to my potential?" and being honest will give you what you need—the fuel to stay on the right track; the ability to make the right decisions. You see, it's not about being perfect and not about beating yourself up; it's about being able to get back up after you fall or after you make a mistake and how willing you are to learn from your mistakes.

The one thing I want you to get from this chapter is the more you focus and strive to be the best you can be, and not only that, focus on truly being honest with yourself, the more opportunities you're going to give yourself to have the right mindset and make the right decisions. A lot of people out there, me being one of them, want to have what we consider success, and we all have our own definition, whether that be providing for our families, giving back to others, living without worrying about stability, or prospering. But are you willing to be honest with yourself? Nobody is going to answer that for you. Nobody is going to accept excuses.

So, right now as you are reading this, I want you to ask yourself: *Am I doing the things I need to do in order for me to be the best person that I can be?* One of the things I did was to take away things that I enjoyed that weren't good for my goals and replace them—not forever, just until I felt I was closer to my goals. If you tell yourself that it's not forever, it makes it a lot easier.

I stopped drinking alcohol—not even one sip—and it was a big contributor to me getting closer to my goals. Once I stopped drinking, I realized my head was clear. I realized how much more I had to give of myself.

I have always been big on reading and listening to audiobooks, and I loved the way this helped me learn more, so I decided instead of listening to music while working out, I would instead listen to audiobooks, which would teach me more and I could spend more time learning from people who I considered successful. There are so many books on successful people—some of my favorite authors are Grant Cardone, Anthony Robbins, and Brendon Burchard—and there are so many more books that are not just career focused but can also help with marriage, parenting, and so much more.

You just need to find what works best for you. Take away unhelpful things you are doing right now that you know you can replace with something that will help you improve on a daily basis. Once I started to replace one habit with another, it was hard for me to go back to the old habit. For example, although I still listen to music from time to time, I now enjoy listening to and learning from audiobooks more, and when I switch back to music, I actually miss the audiobooks. I'm not saying this will happen to you with every substitution that you will make, but I'm sure there are things out there you can start doing that are healthier than your current habits and will contribute more to your success.

Chapter Assignment
- What are three things you are currently doing today that you can replace with a habit that can help get you closer to your goals?

CHAPTER 10:

Fear not Having Fear

Fear is, by definition, from the Merriam-Webster dictionary, is "an unpleasant often strong emotion caused by anticipation or awareness of danger."

We all have different fears, but what we fail to realize is that a lot of our fears are due to our upbringing or things that we worry about that have never happened or won't ever happen.

Fear as Your Servant

I strive to use fear as my servant, rather than my master. Let me give you an example. Some of you may have a fear of jumping out of a plane, dogs, or speaking in front of a large crowd. Now, when you have a fear of doing something, it's a natural thing to not face it because there's a chance it will harm you. But, if you are aware that 95 percent of the time, the outcome you fear is not reality, you will be able to run towards it, rather than away from it.

Now, that doesn't mean that if you have a fear of jumping out of a plane that you should go out and jump out of a plane. No, what I am talking about has to do more with common sense. The fear I am talking about its understanding reality by acknowledging that what you're feeling that may in fact not be reality but rather the working of your subconscious mind. What distinguishes successful people from the rest is that when they face their fears head on. A lot of people out there fear failure, meaning they fear the things they need to do because they feel even if they do them, they will fail. For me, the spice of life, the thing that I like, is competing. So, if I am competing against fear, then I want to win. So, for me, when I fear something, that is an indicator that I need to do it or run towards it. For example, I wouldn't say I feared going on TV, but when asked to go on TV to do an interview, did I fear it? My answer would be yes. But did I run away from it? No, I did not. I simply ran towards it, not thinking about it to the point that I fear didn't have time to alter my decision. At the time I was asked to go on TV, I also had a coworker go on with me, and he was very fearful. I witnessed his fear from beginning to end. The thing that I noticed is not the fear itself but really the things that he was telling himself and the questions he was asking himself.

He asked me, "How come you aren't nervous? Have you done this before? Did you prepare the things that you are going to say?" He then proceeded to tell me that he spent all night preparing. He brought out a three- or four-page long document with all the questions he anticipated being asked so he could be prepared.

When showed me this, I simply told him, "No, I have not gone on TV before, and no I have not prepared for the questions that they are going to ask me, and the reason isn't that I don't want to be prepared, but I have been preparing for moments like these or anything else that comes my way already." I continued, "I know you are scared and nervous, but in order to get through it, you need to lie to yourself. You're afraid, which is an indicator that you are already lying to yourself, telling yourself all of the things that could go wrong. So, if you are going to lie to yourself, make it to your benefit. You see, you could lie to yourself before doing something like going on TV and say to yourself, 'I've done this a million times before, and I am going to do the things I have always done. If anything, they should feel privileged to have me on their show, as I am very knowledgeable.' "

The Wow Factor

What I was doing there was telling him how he should focus his mindset because at that moment that was what I was doing. Which lie do you think would give you the advantage in this situation: "I'm going to fumble my words and sound like an idiot," or "I've done this a million times"? The latter, although still a lie, will help you build up your ego and your confidence.

It sounds like an easy answer; it even sounds like common sense. That's because it is common sense! It goes back to choices that we make, and I am a big believer on knowing that for every action we take, there is a reaction. So, you could take action on the things you fear head on rather than taking action by running away from your fear; either way you are going to get results.

Weather these results end up being good or bad, you want to put yourself in the best position to get you what you want. So, again, when you have fear, you are going to have to ask yourself: *Do I want fear to be my master or my servant?* Now, at that moment, if you cannot overcome your fear, then you have to just jump in the water. What I mean by that is let go. Put yourself in an uncomfortable position.

Stop focusing on the results of how good you will or will not do but rather go out and bomb or fail like no one else has done before. I know that sounds silly, but the truth is that you are likely going to be fine, and if anything, that fear is the result of all the times before that you did not take action but ran away. The fear of failure stopped you from getting what you wanted.

So, take a moment to think about the things that you want and what fears they bring you. How are you going to win by taking action rather than not taking action? Doing the things that you know are going to put yourself in a better position, whether you fail or succeed, is better than doing nothing, even if you do fail.

The Matador Effect

I want you to think about a time where you felt scared or afraid of something and you went ahead and you moved forward and did not turn your back on it. Even though you didn't want to do that very thing, you did it anyway. It doesn't necessarily mean you have to be shaking-in-your-boots afraid or the boogeyman is going to jump out of the closet kind of afraid. But I want you to use your common sense being afraid. Meaning, if you are afraid to give that client bad news because you are concerned if you give that bad news they will cancel, even though you know it's the right thing to do, then yes, you need to be alert and aware at that moment that you are afraid because that is your conscious mind or intuition, whatever you want to call it, your jiminy cricket telling you to get your ass in gear and do the right thing.

I am not saying that you should create situations where you feel fear; what I am saying is if you are like me, and you study many of the greats and many of the successful people out there, you will read or hear that they never run away from fear and they do not let fear control them, rather treat fear like their little bitch. Whenever I fear something, I go at it like a bull going at a matador flinging a red cape. I don't want to analyze it, or mull it over; I don't want feed my fear with waiting because the longer you wait, the more your chances go up of you not acting but running away, which at that point fear has treated you like its little bitch. It's just like with anything; what I mean by that is if you see something as being bad and you feel as if you are better off ignoring it, then what's going to happen is your subconscious mind is going to build what I call a negative muscle. What I mean by that is when you turn your back on making that video because you are scared of what others will think or don't leave a job because you are fearful that if you leave that job you will fail.

I'm not saying to go out and quit your job, nor am I saying to go empty out your bank account and be fearless and play the Lotto. My "disclaimer" here is that with everything that I'm saying, I want you to use your common sense. I use that phrase a lot because even though a lot of things I say sound as if you should know this by now, I've found that's not always the case. There are a lot of people out there who choose not to use their common sense. I want to be honest with you, though, I grew up being told constantly to use my common sense by my dad.

He would go out of his way also to tell me that 98 percent of people out there don't use their common sense. I'm not saying he was right or wrong; I'm simply saying that most of us out there know right from wrong. A lot of times we still choose to do things that we know are wrong, and our common sense tells us it's wrong to either say or do, but we still choose to ignore our common sense. Just like everything that I have said before, you are never going to be perfect. Just like I am writing this book right now, going over common sense, I will be the first person to tell you this: I don't always listen to my common sense. But am I aware of it? Do I acknowledge it? The answer for both of those questions is yes.

Now, I want to tie this all together. Everything always comes back to you providing your clients the "Wow Factor." It's not that easy for everyone to make their clients experience the "Wow Factor." I'm sure you've heard this before, but I will say it again: "If it was easy, then everyone would do it." In fact, the reason I decided to write about this is because the "Wow Factor" was created because most people don't provide or do the things they need to do, so much that when you actually do the things you need to do for your clients, you go the extra mile and you tell them the things they need to hear, they are surprised. They cannot believe you answered your phone at nine o'clock at night! They cannot believe that you met them on a Sunday!

Now, I want to stop and say that to attain the "Wow Factor" doesn't mean neglecting t your family or neglecting other things that you need to do just to do whatever your clients want you to do all the time.

There will be times where you will receive that phone call on a Saturday at 6:00 a.m., and you will look over and ask, *Should I answer it. They have some nerve calling on a Saturday.... I will call them later.... I will call them back on Monday.* You then decide to sleep, in and the next thing you know, Monday comes around, and you call that client back, and the client has thought about your proposal all weekend long. They needed to talk with you simply because they were stressed out and ultimately decided not to move forward with your proposal. What would most people think about that? If that happened to you, what would you say to yourself? You might make an excuse up or feel that it's not you; it's the client. I want you to know—and this is something that I did not make up nor did the people that I learned it from makeup—in order for you to grow as a person, you have to never blame others; always blame yourself for how you could have done things differently. I will say nine out of ten times the answer is not far away, and it will pop in your head right away. You will think, *Why didn't I just answer the phone? Why didn't I just call them later?*

The Wow Factor

Again, some of the things I'm saying pertain to business, as a lot of this stuff that happened to us. Yes, I would still say to you, when something bad happens to me, I don't go around just saying, "It's my fault... It's my fault." You cannot simply go through the motions with anything if you are being true to yourself and you really want to grow. The best way I can put it is if you do something half-assed, you're going to get half-assed results. We have all experienced it. Right now, you can more than likely sit back and think about some of the times you decided to take a shortcut or to do something half-assed and you suffered the consequences.

So, the next time you are fearful of something, or the next time you don't want to do something, even though it could come back and bite you in the ass later, I want you to use what I call the matador effect. The matador effect is where you don't think about it and you see red and you charge forward. You act fearless.

Chapter Assignment

- What is something you can do to get out of your comfort zone? I'm not talking about cliff diving or dancing along a moving car but something that is real where you can go for now.
- Write down how fear can be a good thing and some ways you use it for your benefit.

CHAPTER 11:

Listen to Your Gut Feeling

Don't Sugar Coat It

I think everyone has what is called "intuition" or a "gut feeling," but many of us choose to ignore it or pretend it isn't there. You may be wondering how this relates to sales and customer service, so let me give you an example. Let's say you have bad news that you need to give to a client. Typically, when this situation rears its head, we start thinking of all the different ways we can deliver the message while not looking like a bad person. The fact is, if your gut tells you to tell this person the bad news, and you know it is something they need to hear, then you need to be as brutally honest as you can and not try and sugar coat it or say it in a way that makes you look good. If anything, I feel that a lot of people in sales try and sugar coat what they say to their clients, and the effect of sugar coating has the opposite effect, as that is not what the clients wants. They want the same thing you and I would want, which is the truth and nothing but the truth, and they can handle it. However, most salespeople tell a client, little by little, the things they feel they want to hear because they are too scared the client will get upset if it's bad news, ultimately resulting in losing the sale.

The fact is, you cannot lose something you do not have. Meaning you don't have that transaction unless you close it. Period. So why be concerned about losing it? The best thing to do is to be brutally honest and tell your clients exactly what is happening, even if it means you messed up big time and you are the one to blame. What that's going to do is at that moment is, yes, your client will be upset, and yes, your client will be upset *with you* in that moment, but that will wear off, and what you will get is more trust with that client. When I have bad news for a client, I do not wait. I do not allow myself feed what we call fear. A lot of times, overcoming fear just involves not overthinking or over analyzing it.

For example, when your gut starts to tell you to go and work out, and you start thinking about working out, what happens? The longer you wait, the more reasons you come up with to not work out. You start to get ready, and you start to ask yourself questions. You start getting upset that you don't have the perfect workout gear. You then say to yourself that you can always work out later on that evening. So, at that point, you start to let doubt and reluctance get the best of you.

It can be overwhelming to allow doubt, reluctance, and even fear to control us versus just going with our instincts. Now, of course, we all have fears. I have to always remind myself that the best thing to do is it move forward. By always focusing on moving forward, it shifts my mindset in a way that does not allow fear or doubt to have a buffet to allow it to grow. Now, don't get me wrong, I experience times where I allow fear or doubt to either win or get the best of me, but the difference is not letting that fear have more wins than you.

So, the next time you have a client to whom you have to give bad news, I want you to take a moment and think about all the times you were in that situation. I want you to ask yourself, *If someone had bad news for me, would I want them to either tell me the truth, or sugar coat it, or to soften the blow by saying it in a way that I can understand but not get overwhelmed?*

You see, whenever you say something truthful to someone, they might respond negatively; they may be being momentarily stubborn, ignorant, or refuse to believe reality. That's okay; we all fall into this. It's still better to get that reaction out of the way than to be somewhat dishonest by sugar coating the truth because people can pick up subconsciously that you aren't being fully honest.

You Can Still "Soften the Blow"

This doesn't mean you can't soften the blow. When you're about to give someone bad news, and you "soften the blow," that means you can cushion the reaction. For example, you have to tell a client that you cannot help them with purchasing their home because they do not have enough to either put down or they have too much debt. So, when you are about to call that person and let them know the situation, you want to first say it in a way that has also a positive outcome. What I mean by that is you are not the reason that they have too much debt, and you are not the reason that the lender requires less debt. So, what you want to do is tell them that you have several solutions to a challenge that the client may have. I never say the word "problem." I don't like using that word because to me anything that happens that does not allow you or your clients to get what they want or what they need is simply a challenge. At that point, they have to do one of two things: they have to either retreat and/or deny it or face that challenge.

Tackling Challenges

Your client will feel more comfortable with a leader who is honest and resourceful rather than one who is dishonest and lacks flexibility to deal with challenges. When you are working with somebody, you are put in a position to have all the qualities that you would want in someone if they were, let's say, taking care of your kids or working on your car. So, whatever it is you are doing for your clients, you need to always be coming up with solutions, and the best way to overcome fear and not let challenges get in your way is to always be better safe than sorry.

The reality of the situation is that when you are presenting something to a client, yes, it is not your fault that they have bills; yes, it is not your fault that they have a lower-than-ideal income; but it IS your fault that YOU were put in that situation with them. You have to always have to have the mindset that everything that happens to you is your fault unless you do not want to grow—whether it be spiritually, or physically, or professionally, or as a father, mother, brother, or sister. If you're reading this book, I'll bet you're like me and like to win at anything you do. Now, I have met a lot of people who simply don't mind losing; they go through life in what I call a fog.

Having a Reason

I can recall a time that my company wanted me to talk to our team to go over some things that I felt made me strive to achieve more in our industry. I was very eager to communicate something that would hopefully help or assist my team to improve production. I knew right away what I was going to ask my team, which was a simple question.

I went to the meeting the next day, and I simply asked everyone to individually answer the question: "Why are you here?" And that was it.

As we went around the room, it was amazing to hear the responses that we received from each individual. The reactions from 80 percent of the people around the table were shock. They were dumbfounded and acted as if it was a trick question. Here are some of the responses that I received: "I'm here to make money." This was a simple response but logical, I guess. "I'm here for my family to provide for them." Again, this was a logical response but one I felt they gave because they thought that's what I wanted to hear.

What was interesting was the response of one of the employees there who was not doing well; in fact, he was on the verge of being let go. I liked this guy a lot. When it came to his turn to answer the question, he looked lost. He did not know what to say. In fact, it was quite awkward for everybody. He almost looked like he was upset that I was asking him this question, which, at the time, blew my mind that someone could be somewhere but not really have a reason to be there. He simply did not know what to say. So, after being silent for a while and having the look of wheels spinning and turning, he then said that he was there for his dogs. Everyone around the room had looks of confusion and disbelief.

I simply said, "Okay," and moved on.

So, throughout the room, we noticed that the 20 percent who were doing really well in the company seemed excited to give their answers These responses were inspiring and well thought out, and in many cases, these people had a written plan or goal of what they wanted to accomplish and how being at that company was going to get them where they wanted to be. The point of me telling you this is that if you don't have a reason why—not only that, a good, better-than-average, extraordinary, do-or-die, all-or-nothing reason why—you are doing what you do, then it will reflect in your production, or results, or accomplishments in anything and everything that you do, good or bad. Now, when I say good or bad, that's simply what it is. Maybe you highly have a passion and you love to play video games, and you spend hours, if not days, if not years, thinking about it, studying it, physically playing on your PlayStation 4.

Another example is, let's say, that you are passionate about doing drugs, or drinking alcohol, or doing anything that is bad for you. If somebody asked you, "Why do you do that?" You're probably not doing to say, "I don't know." The person who answers honestly will say, "I'm doing it because I think it about it every day." You see, if you step back and look at both positive and negative scenarios, people who are passionate have similar responses, regardless of what they are doing. They think about what they are doing all day every day. They obsess over it. Whether what you are doing is helpful or harmful, it requires the same amount of attention. It requires action. It requires a "why."

Let's say you are a hoarder, and someone is to describe you. They say you don't do anything and just sit around in a house full of junk. You are lazy; you don't have a passion for life. You need help.

Some of you out there might know someone who you consider a hoarder. they You may or may not feel the same way, but the fact is that person is not lazy; they are passionate; they do have a meaning in life; they simply have the meaning of life misdirected, which results in harm to themselves and those around them. You see, they are not lazy—how did they get all that junk in their house? Someone had to pick it up and bring it in. It didn't just magically appear. Someone had to place it in that spot, and that requires work. So how can you call that person lazy? They are simply having their resources that they were given misdirected in a harmful or negative way.

So, the guy with dog came up to me after the meeting and asked me if I would go out to lunch with him because he wanted to speak with me. I told him, "Yes, I would love to go." I could tell it was important to him, so I said, "Let's go right now."

The Wow Factor

At lunch, he told me he wanted to thank me for talking with him and wanted to get my advice. He also said he wanted to explain the answer he gave during the meeting. He then proceeded to tell me that when I asked him that question, he was in somewhat of a state of shock. He had simply been going through life, avoiding asking himself that question, and when I asked him that question, he realized that he needed to have a "why" and realized it was very bad. He said he felt lost and like he wasted all this time not having a higher purpose in life.

He then proceeded to tell me that he was having problems at home and his girlfriend would pick up stray dogs and bring them home and that it was getting to the point where his house was filled with urine and feces throughout. He said he had been trying to get his girlfriend, who he did love, to get rid of some of the animals, as they were keeping him up at night. It had gotten to a point where he didn't even sleep in his own bed next to his girlfriend—a dog had taken his spot on the bed. When he would go and try to lie down, the dog would growl at him.

I asked, "What do you plan on doing?"

He said, "I don't know. That's why I asked you to go to lunch with me—to give me advice because I am lost."

Now, I want to say that I gave him advice, and he went on to do great things, but that simply is not the case. I did tell him he needed to first reevaluate what he wanted and needed to make some drastic changes, and the first one was demanding that the dogs be found a home that was suitable, not only for their wellbeing but for his. If that didn't work, he needed to take the initiative to either find another place to live or ask her to move out.

He then proceeded to tell me that yes, he did want her to leave, but he was with her for so long that he just couldn't do it.

Then I proceeded to ask him why, and he said because he loved her and they have broken up in the past and have gotten back together, and he did not want to go through that again.

So, I then said, "Well, it sounds to me like you do love her and you want to also make sure that she loves you. So, if she loves you, she's going to work with you and take action on things that are bothering you, like getting rid of some of the animals." Now I'm not a couples' counselor, nor do I pretend to be one. I was simply being a friend giving advice to someone I cared about.

So, after we had lunch, he said he felt much better, and throughout the next several months, I saw a change in his demeanor, and his production went up. I continued to be his friend, and for a period of time, it seemed like things were going really well. However, that is how he started out at the company; he was performing really well, then he fell into a slump.

To end this story, what happened is during the time he was doing well, he ended up asking his girlfriend to leave, and she did in fact leave, and he moved on and started to work on himself. He was feeling good about his life and purpose. However, eventually, she moved back in. They are back together, and now things are going back to the way they were. At one point, I said to him, "No one is going to force you to motivate yourself. Nobody is going to force you to do the things that are good for you nor am I going to have a magical response or set or words for you. Your gut feeling is already telling you what you need to do."

The Wow Factor

Chapter Assignment

- Write down a time you listened to your gut and you realized you were right as well as a time you didn't listen and wished you had.

CHAPTER 12:

Survive Any Economy by Making Your Own

Mental Preparation

The only way anyone can provide the "Wow Factor" to their clients is to be prepared mentally. Some of the things you can do to mentally prepare are basic but key elements that our gut already tells us to do.

For example, you already know you should work out at least once a day—find something you love to do that involves getting your heartbeat up and allows you to stay active. What I do is play basketball almost every morning, I like set my alarm to get up at 3:30 a.m. so that I can have time to wake up write down my goals for that day and my future as well as get ready and drive to the gym. I like to be at the gym before 5:00 a.m., right when it opens. When my editor read this, she wanted to make sure this was correct—and I don't blame her! It seems early to get to the gym by 5:00 a.m., and it is. I don't do it every morning, but that is always my goal.

If I wanted to, I could wake up at 11:00 a.m., but when I wake up late, I feel horrible all day, I feel like I showed up late to the party. Also, I wake up early because my wife gets up early and leaves early to take the kids to school, and I like to surprise her by buying her Starbucks and getting the kids a croissant. If I get up early, I might get to spend time with my kids and say goodbye to them before she drives them to school.

You might be thinking, *That's crazy talk*, and maybe you're right. However, think about it differently. Why do I do this? I do it because most people do not; instead, they do what society considers the norm, and the fact is, if you keep doing things that everyone else does, but you wanted to be special—you want to live up to your potential, you want to have the perfect marriage, career, body, you want to be a good Dad, etc.—just know it's not going to be easy. In fact, it will require A LOT of your time and effort. Yes, it will require work and dedication, persistence, a positive attitude, patience, and organization. These are all things that successful people have cultivated. I'm not reinventing the wheel. I'm saying I know what works for me.

I know that if I have this level of mental preparation and drive, even 30 percent of the time, it will still be more than most. So, again, just because you strive to do more, give more, and be the best you can be does not mean you will be perfect, or you will not have bad days. But the more you do it, the less those bad days will hurt you, as by focusing on having days you consider an 8 or a 9 out of 10, the more your success rate rises. For me, waking up early has many benefits, like I get to spend more time with my family because it seems as if there are more hours in the day. It helps me tremendously to sleep better, and not only that, it makes me go to bed early as well. Again, how bad do you want it? Really, you need to start by asking yourself how badly you want to transform your life.

Another example, which I do every day and you can do too, is that I give myself a numerical rating on how well I did throughout the whole day the following day. I base that number on a scale from 1 – 10, in which 10 would be a perfect day. I suggest you sit down and write out your perfect day and make it as challenging as possible in order to make a 10 very hard to get.

Understand that successful people are successful because they create habits over time that allow them to be disciplined in everything aspect of their life, whether it's work, family, hobbies and anything they can help improve who they are or who they want to be.

Mental Strength

What exactly is mental strength? I do not want you to mistake it for ignoring the obvious or sweeping things under the rug, hoping your challenges go away.

The way you work out any muscle is to do things make you feel discomfort. When you have these feelings, that is your body and mind telling you that you need to do that very thing, or you will not grow. And the truth is, after you do that thing you were putting off because you felt you would experience discomfort, you will realize that you were very wrong, and if anything, you felt as if a lot of pressure was taken off of you. In fact, it feels good when you do something that you would normally ignore to deal with another day.

You hear it a lot: we all go through the same struggles. This is somewhat true and somewhat false. The reason we all have unique or different struggles is obvious; we have different upbringings, social environments, and so forth. But the fact is, we all do not react the same to our challenges of life, whether it be not making the team, getting a bad grade, having something tragic happen to you, or feeling lost. But the fact is, no matter what happens, there is someone in the world that has had it happen to them, and they were able to bounce back in a very successful and positive way. So, knowing that, you have to ask yourself if the things you're going through right now are going to get better if you continue to dwell on it. Should you instead take action and focus on the present and the future? Ask yourself, "How will I ever know how strong I can be unless I face my challenges head on?"

Distinguish Yourself

Take this level of fortitude and dedication to whatever you do. Do things that others won't. On my clients' birthdays, I call them, email them, and I get them a card, personally writing out a sincere birthday note.

These are small examples of doing what others, which will help you provide the "Wow Factor" and stay in business.

You have to stay sharp, eat well, work out, learn something new every day, and do things to create value, such as, create videos, write blogs, start your own podcast…the possibilities are endless.

Why do I do all of these things, both for myself and for my clients? Because I like making people feel good. I like being different. I like to stand out from the crowd. I always like doing what others won't in order to give the "Wow Factor."

Chapter Assignment

- Ask yourself: "What would my perfect day be?" Be very specific memorize it until you know the events like the back of your hand.
- How bad do you want to be successful, and what are you willing to do without compromising your morals?

CHAPTER 13:

Confidence Is Key

In this chapter I am going to be going over I feel is one of the most important things any individual will need in order to reach what I call "The Zone." What I'm talking about is confidence. The thing you have to understand—and I don't want to say this lightly—is if you do not believe in you, then how can anyone else believe in your abilities.

Now I'm not talking about being arrogant or acting as if you know more than everybody in the room. What I'm talking about is something that nobody can give to you, meaning there is no magic pill for it. It is that simple; you either have it or you don't. Now I do also want to say that confidence isn't something that you just conjure up in your mind and is something that you make up; confidence is a series of actions done over and over to the point it spills out into the world. Let me give you an example. If you started a sport, such as basketball, which is my favorite sport, you and I both know that somebody who has been playing for 10 years compared to somebody who just started is going to have a lot more confidence in their abilities to dominate either you or other opponents.

Now, I don't want you to misconstrue what I mean by that, as it makes no difference whether you've been playing basketball for 10 years or one; the difference is what that person does on a daily basis to dominate their profession. So, if you just started off playing basketball, and your goal is to, let's say, be rookie of the year because you feel that reaching for a championship may be too high of a reach, I would disagree with that very much; the reason being is that a lot of our limitations or setbacks have to do with what society deems you to either be or become based upon their beliefs.

So, sticking with this example, if you just started, let's say, your first year in the NBA and your goal is to be Rookie of the Year, and you have another player on your team, and their goal is to win a championship their first year, then ultimately the person who has a higher reach is going to perform more actions on a daily basis in order to reach their desired goal. Both individuals are either going to reach their goals or they are going to fall short of their goals if not taking the necessary actions in order for them to reach their destinations.

Let's say the person who is reaching to achieve more, a championship in their first year, falls short of their goal, but they become Rookie of the Year. Compare this with you, whose goal was to be Rookie of the Year. If you fall short of this goal, you get nothing.

My point again is you have to put yourself always in a state of domination in order to be more than what everyone else feels or doesn't feel you should be. The only way you're going to do that is having a belief every day, and the way to have that belief is by taking big actions to build your confidence higher and higher. The thing that I always noticed when I was growing up in high school, which I'm sure a lot of you have noticed as well, is that the individuals who had everything going for them, as far as their athletic abilities and number of years playing the sport, were not always the best players. I never felt that I was the worst player on the team; if anything, I always felt that my abilities and skill level was better than everyone else's on my team. That didn't mean that I was technically the best player on the team; it simply means I was selling myself every day, every second, that I was the best player, not only on my team, but in my entire league.

What you need to do, on a daily basis, is make sure your beliefs aren't small beliefs; you need to make them huge beliefs. You will that notice people who end up being a lot more successful than what others deemed them to be comes from the fact that through all their wins and through all their failures, their belief never faltered.

I know that this is something that is easier said than done. You're going to have times where you beat yourself up, and I want to say that when that happens, it's okay. All that means is that you are human, and all that means is that you want more out of life and you are positively dissatisfied with not completing your goal.

As I'm writing this book, I know that I am not where I want to be, and others may have a belief that I should be happy with what I have. Now, that statement should really hit home to anybody that wants more out of life and is putting themselves in a situation to where they have or will receive criticism. The best way I can put it is, if you are wanting more out of your abilities and you have high beliefs and high goals, then you're simply going to have to have a mindset that does not alter your reality. To simplify it, when you hear any negative comments or you receive negative feedback from anybody—meaning it could be your best friend, the cashier at the gas station, or even your own mom—you need to always see that as fuel for your beliefs. There's not one successful individual who went through life and crawled, scraped, and had that never giving up, gotta-never-quit-Rudy mentality who would tell you that they never had naysayers and, if you're going to listen to everyone that tells you how to do something, or when to do something, or you should change this, or you should change that, you will never give yourself the opportunity to be the person that you ultimately want to be.

Now, by no means am I saying to not take advice and to throw darts in a dark room blindfolded; what I'm saying is that in order for you to truly maximize your capabilities, you're going to have to have setbacks, or failures, or missed opportunities in order for you to grow. I really feel that the fire within me is not something that I was born with but is something that I continuously feed on a daily basis. In order to feed the drive and motivation and the gotta-have-it mentality, you first have to start the fire, and then you have to continuously feed that fire. The only way you are going to make that fire bigger and keep it burning is to take necessary actions on a daily basis, and when I say daily, I don't mean Monday through Friday business hours; I mean it has to be an obsession that consumes you to the point where before you go to bed you think about it, you dream about it, you wake up, and you constantly have a smirk on your face because you know nothing or no one will stop you.

It doesn't mean that you won't have setbacks, or that somebody won't throw you off track and even succeed in stopping you, as that will happen. The difference between the successful and the unsuccessful is not what happens to them, but how they react to it. Again, I don't want to write words that make it seem that I am perfect or that you have to be perfect and you have to walk around like a robot being Mr. Positive. The fact of the matter is you will be faced with challenges more and more, and as your success grows, your challenges will only be bigger and will require more mental strength.

So, with that being said, you have to go at it as if you welcome the challenges that come your way, and not only that, you have to learn from your failures. The only way to learn from your failures is to move forward. You're going to beat yourself up, and you're going to have bad days, which is normal, but successful people don't dwell on it too long, and they always keep moving.

I've read a lot of books on the subject, and people who are successful typically say one thing: If they could go back in time, they would not wait to be what they considered successful; they would act as if they were already successful so that they could document their rise to the top from that perspective.

I want you to understand that confidence is not something that you are born with, nor is it something that you can fake; it is simply compounding daily actions and daily successes that eventually overflow as a result.

Chapter Assignment

- What activities are you doing right now that are not helping you get closer to your goals? What can you can you do to replace that activity that can help you get closer to your goals?
- What are some beliefs you tell yourself on a daily basis that can be negative and what is a positive example you can replace it with? For example, if you said you do not have enough experience to be successful right now, then replace that thought with *I am the right person because I am experienced, and I will continue to get better every day.* Again, even if you're not experienced, do not let that stop you, as an excuse is something you tell yourself to justify actions.

CHAPTER 14:

Do the Right Thing

At the end of the day, if you don't do the right thing, you will never be successful.

Now, you may feel I like that sounds harsh, or maybe you totally agree with what I am saying, but I think we would all agree that by doing the right thing, your odds of being the person that you would like others, like your kids, your family, and the people you love, to emulate are better.

When you are rising and you are focused on what you want, you are going to be faced with shortcuts. Now I want to be the first one to tell you that if something sounds too good to be true, and your gut tells you there's something wrong, at this point you should simply run away from whatever it is you are questioning. In other words, if you are questioning something because you feel it sounds good, but you have a lingering thought or feeling that it is not the right thing to do, then you are going to have to use that thing called common sense.

Defining Success

You're going to have to do a lot of things that you don't want to do in order for you to get to where you want to go and in order for you to be whatever you deem successful. Now the reason I say whatever you deem successful is because everybody's definition of success is different.

My definition of success may not be the same as yours, but from my perspective, success is not a moment, a destination, or a finish line. Success is what you want and where you want to be. Now in order to figure out what success is to you, you simply cannot ignore it or treat it like a bus stop; you have to really put yourself into a mental state, and you need to take it very seriously and ask yourself what is it you really want.

The reason it is so important to take it seriously, to block out time to really define success for yourself, is because when you do this, you may start to realize that what you actually want is not really that hard to get, nor is it going to make you happy, and you may be selling yourself short.

I grew up wanting it all, and I grew up with people around me who had beliefs that wanting it all was not a good thing; if anything, this mindset could be considered selfish or greedy, and someone who wanted it all could come across as arrogant. But, I always felt that to me it didn't matter because I've always known what I want and what I don't want.

Now by me wanting it all, I don't mean I want gold-string shoelaces or a $200,000 watch and Bentley that drives itself. It also doesn't mean I don't want all that because I would take a $2,000 watch! What I'm trying to say is that I have taken the time by studying, listening, and reading hundreds if not thousands of books on success. I've learned from experience and the accounts of others that it doesn't matter how good you are, and it doesn't matter what you want or what you consider success to be if you don't do the right thing. Now, don't get me wrong, there many people out there who don't do the right thing, and you may look at them, and you may even envy them, but it's a mirage. They look as though they are very successful, but these people may be living with guilt for taking shortcuts to where they are or guilt for not doing the right thing. That's not success.

Now I want to give you a brief list of what I consider success or having it all. Now keep in mind as you go through my list, what I consider success could change. When you are thinking about your own definition of success and what you want from life, never limit yourself.

What I want is to be successful at being a good father, being a good husband. I want to be considered somebody who is an asset to others. Success to me is giving, and not just giving to give something back but giving simply because I can. Success is being financially independent so that I may focus on the things that will allow me to live my life in the way that I want. Financial independence allows me to do what I love, which is helping others get what they want.

I realized when I was about eight years old that when you focus on giving for giving's sake, not to receive anything, it makes you feel good and puts you in a natural state of mind. When I say a natural state of mind, I mean that a lot of people believe or have beliefs that we are born sinners, or we all have "I want it all, and I don't want to share" mentality. For me, that's just someone else's beliefs. I think a natural state of mind is one of abundance.

Defining Your Values

When I grew up, I took time to come up with my own beliefs. To me, if you have not come up with your own beliefs, or have not taken the time to understand why you have the beliefs that you have, you are still transitioning—don't take this the wrong way—from childhood to adulthood. The reason I say that is because I feel that just because you get older, does not automatically mean you become a functioning adult who contributes to those around you. It's just like the saying that anyone can have kids, but it doesn't mean that they are automatically a good parent.

It's worth taking the necessary time to come up with what you consider to be right from wrong. Here's an example from my childhood. When I was a kid, I knew that my father's beliefs weren't mine. I wasn't necessarily the smartest kid in the world, but I didn't lack intelligence either. To me, this was simply a personality trait that I had. If you grew up idolizing your father, or mother, or someone else who took care of you and adopted their beliefs, this is very common. Also, understand that if you don't know something is right or wrong, or you're not aware because you've never thought about it or even thought to think about it, that's normal. It's okay to not know, but you should take the time to educate yourself, to do things to help yourself grow. If you don't, it essentially handicaps you.

So, as you are reading this book right now, you may be having some thoughts about all the beliefs that were placed upon you or you may be starting to realize you never really took the time to come up with your own beliefs—you simply adopted those of the people around you who you loved and cared about. So, now that you know this, you have to use your common sense and analyze which beliefs you have right now that you don't necessarily agree with.

Take the time to think about the beliefs you have—about the world, about relationships, about success, about money, about God or spirituality, about raising children, about friendship, etc., and write them down. Then think about *why* each of these is a belief you have. You may come up with five, or ten, or twenty beliefs that you have, and in the process of writing them down and analyzing them, you may start to question and revise those beliefs. For example, I mentioned before that my father believed that when good things happen to you, be careful because that means bad luck is around the corner. He also believed that money should be spent abundantly and that it would never run out. He also hated Mondays and felt that in order to become wealthy, you have to work harder. Now, I want to say right away that working harder by no means is a bad thing; I would say his beliefs about working harder were something that I believed, and I idolized him, as he was a hard worker and provided for his family. However, I would not say that simply working harder will get you the results that you want. The reason I say that is we live now in a society where we don't get paid on efforts but yet we are judged on our results. I believe that my dad was a good man, but he simply adopted his parents' beliefs. I chose not to.

You're going to have to be honest with yourself when you go over some of your beliefs and behaviors and ultimately decide if they are right or wrong. Only you will know if you are being honest with yourself.

Do the right thing and take stock of your beliefs. Understand that temptation will be there, but there are no shortcuts, and there is no magic pill for success. Only you know what success means to you, but never be ashamed of wanting to be successful at everything. Whether you want to be a successful mother, father, wife, husband, brother, sister, aunt, cousin or businessperson.

I would encourage to go somewhere where you can peacefully write your thoughts with no distractions and write down what success means to you. And all the pleasure you will have by accomplishing this success. Also write down all the pain you will experience by not accomplishing this success. That is what keeps me pushing more and more. This is something that will not only motivate you but will also expand the capacity of the way you act and think, as your vision of success will determine your actions.

Chapter Assignment

- Write down in detail what your own definition of success is and exactly what it means to you. Try and write down all the emotions you would feel if you were successful, as well as how it would make your loved ones feel as well.

CHAPTER 15:

Focus on the Root, not the Fruit

In this chapter I want to go over a main key element for success, which cannot be something you fake but something you have to dig deep to find and keep.

Let's face it—a lot of people in sales are in sales to earn an unlimited amount of income rather than have to clock in or clock out and have a cutoff. You earn in relation to how much you do. If you started off in the sales industry with that in mind, just know that is normal and you're not alone.

I do want to say, however, that after reading this chapter, you can no longer continue to think this way or have this focus. If you continue to hold onto this mindset, you are not being true to yourself or your family, and your success, if any, will be short lived. If that struck a nerve, then good because the truth usually does. I know you are not reading this book for me to tell you what you want to hear but for me to tell you what you need to hear. The first thing I want to go over is that there is no way you are working just for a piece of green paper or numbers on a screen, as they are not real. What is real is helping others and having that drive and focus, knowing if you do good things then good things will and do eventually happen; it just may not be exactly when you want or need it to be.

Asking the Right Questions

I feel the only way to focus on the right thing and to learn to not focus on the negative is to continue to ask yourself the right questions. In order to ask the right questions, you need to dig very deep into your "why," and after coming up with some answers, then you need to keep digging until you find your gold. Simply doing something once or twice will never be enough, as you will need to continue to ask yourself why you are doing what you're doing—whether you are working out, helping a client at work, or doing something as simple as reading a book, in order to maximize your results in the shortest time.

For example, before you go to work out, sit down and take a couple of deep breaths and ask yourself, *Why am I going to go and work out right now?* If you find yourself calling bullshit on yourself when you answer, *to continue to look good*, simply ask yourself again, digging a little deeper. Sometimes this means adding a little more to your question. For example, ask, W*hy am I working out? Why am I driving to the gym when I could be relaxing at home?* Asking the right questions with everything you do and being honest with yourself will ultimately pull at your heartstrings, and if it does not, then you're either not being honest with yourself or you are asking the wrong questions. The reason for this is that we have knee-jerk responses or reactions, and nine out of ten times, if you answer something quickly, without looking inside, it's not how you actually feel.

Also understand that this book is about more than just providing your clients excellent service; it has to do with all aspects of your life. You are reading this book because you want to provide your clients the type of service that makes them think of you more than another salesperson who is helping them with their transaction. So instead of pretending to be all the things your clients want and need, why not be that person and much, much more by taking control of all avenues in your life so that anyone you meet will know that you're not only someone they can trust but that when they're dealing with you, they're dealing with the best of the best.

The Wow Factor

Chapter Assignment

- Write down your reasons "why" you want to be successful in detail. An example would be a want to be wealthy. But why? The paper or the number does nothing. What will you do with your wealth?

CHAPTER 16:

Listen to What They Don't Say

I would say, 80 percent of the time, when someone is discussing something, it isn't so much what they say but what they don't say that matters most. If you're unfamiliar with reading between the lines, or if you think you are unaware of what is going on behind the scenes, let me give you an example that I think will make you realize you are more aware than you think. Think about an instance where you've been talking to someone, and it's almost as if you can finish their sentence. This level of listening is not as easy as it sounds; listening and interpreting what someone is saying beyond what they are verbally saying is just like working out a muscle. Someone who is very attuned to what a person is saying can even interpret what another person *really means* when they are saying something different.

For example, let's say that you are married, and your wife tells you that she was thinking about a dress that she was going to get but she didn't really like the color on her.

At that point, if you're verbally hearing what she is saying and you take what she is saying at face value, you may ask, "Well what color is it"?

Now, at that point, she may give you a color, say, she says, "yellow," but she may also be thinking *Wow, there is a color out there that he thinks I look bad, or ugly, in.*

Most of you reading this or listening to this probably think, *And what's wrong with that?* It may not be that bad, and you may not have a disagreement, and you may not end up in the dog house, or you may. But this is a prime example of reading between the lines. She said, "I like the dress, but I don't think the color would look that good on me." You heard what she said, but if you had exceptional listening skills, you may have interpreted that to mean, "I like a dress; however, when I tried it on, it made me feel ugly, and I felt you would not like the dress on me because yellow makes me look ugly." So, if that's the way you heard it, you would likely respond in a more compassionate, meaningful way.

Being an exceptional listener is a skill that nobody will ever completely perfect, but it can be improved upon. The more you focus on truly listening to what someone is saying, the better you will become. It's going to carry over not only in your business but also with your everyday life, weather you're dealing with your wife, your kids, or your boss.

To go back to the example, if you are listening, you would say, "I am not sure what color that dress is, but you would look beautiful in any color, Sugar Plum." She would then look at you with loving eyes, and at that point she would be more open to whatever you have to say.

Let's say that you saw the dress that she was talking about and you felt she did in fact look beautiful in that dress, or just as an example, you felt the color was really not her color. Either way, it doesn't matter because you are putting yourself in a much better position than you would be by just saying, "Well, what color was it?" Now, I don't want you to misinterpret what I am saying at all as being manipulative because I will be the first one to say I am highly against being manipulative. But what I am highly for is the very reason you are reading this book, which is better communication. What I mean is, if you are communicating better by being a better listener, that would not mean you are manipulating someone, but what it would mean that you are taking the time to understand someone.

The Wow Factor

So, when I'm going over these examples, I want you to understand that this is how you're going to go the extra mile and give the what I call the "Wow Factor." The "Wow Factor" has to do with you going above and beyond, doing more then what is expected of you. The "Wow Factor" is not you kissing your boss's butt, or pretending to listen, or telling someone something that you feel will help you get your way. That would be wrong, and you could come across as untrustworthy.

I frequently go to eat at Wings N' Things, which is one of my favorite places for buffalo wings and have been going to the same place for years. I'm sure you can think of somewhere similar in your life. Wherever you go, I want you to start to notice how some of the people that are employed there treat you. For example, I have been going to the same place to buy the wings that I like for years, and I have noticed the difference in someone who has a positive attitude and the ability to listen to me when I place my order verses somebody who I can tell does not want to be there and cannot wait to go home. They don't listen, and every time they take your order, it almost makes you cringe inside from discomfort. So, why is that? Why is it that two people have completely separate outlooks on where they work and how they treat their customers? It's because they have different outlooks.

It's almost like finding a diamond in the rough to see someone who is positive, a good listener, and happy to take your order. I can sit here and tell you all the reasons why that is, but that's not the point; it's irrelevant. The fact is, there's a small percentage out there who take pride in every single thing that they do. However, there is a large percentage of people out there that do not take pride in everything that they do, and it could be anything, from where they work, how they are as a brother, or a sister, or even a friend. They just simply go through life one day at a time. Those are the people you will have a conversation with and will be able to tell they aren't listening; they are simply waiting for their turn to talk. Now, I'm talking about the extremes right now, but I think you see my point.

If you are reading or listening to this book, I know you want more out of life. You want to be better and improve at everything that you do. So, the whole point of this chapter is that if you want to be a better listener, start by listening to anyone you have a conversation with on a daily basis, to the point where they as you, "Are you listening?" Meaning don't respond, and don't talk until they go out of their way to ask you to respond. At first, it's going to feel weird; it may even feel silly to you, or even at first come across as awkward, or even rude. Again, as I said earlier, it's just like working out a muscle, and weather you go to the gym or you don't go to the gym, we all know that when you start something new or start working out after a long period of inactivity, it feels awkward in the beginning. It's going to feel like riding a bike for the first time. You need to work at it and keep at it.

So, the next time someone says, "Hello, were you listening?" "Hello, McFly, anyone home?" I want you to say "Yes, before I talk, I just wanted to be sure you were done telling me how you feel." Now, that doesn't mean going around pretending to listen, waiting for them to say, "Are you listening?" What I am saying is, start off by keeping it simple. The more you truly try to be a good listener, the more results you will have. By being cognizant of it, you're going to put yourself in a much better position than someone who just doesn't give a damn, who just doesn't care whether their listening skills are improving or not improving. We all make mistakes. I sometimes catch myself not listening to a client, or my wife may catch me not listening to her. It's something I'm practicing every day, and so can you. You will catch more honey by listening, and you will get stung by a swarm of bees by not listening.

Chapter Assignment

- Try to see how long you can listen to someone talk to you without responding until they say, "Are you listening?" Tell them, "Yes," and let them know you didn't want to interrupt them because you were making sure to listen to what they had to say.

CHAPTER 17:

Make a Friend, not a Commission Check

I'm sure a lot of you out there have had experience working with someone who was either referred to you or was a good friend or family member and you felt like you could just be yourself.

A lot of salespeople, when they are reading a book or listening to an audiobook, are trying to find the right words to say. They are looking for that magic pill. The fact is, there is no such thing. You are simply just like the person you are trying to help; you could be in the exact same position where you have the same challenge. So, think about it. Do you talk different when you are given a referral versus when someone hands you a lead and says, "Here, call this person"? Are you trying to close the deal so you can get paid on it and move on to the next one? Are you always trying to go out of your way to find tools that will allow you to speak less to the client, so that you can help more clients and not spend more time with your current clients? Now, I'm not saying at all that you should go out of your way to spend time with a client just for the sake of spending time with them. What I am saying is if you are focused on having a normal conversation rather than waiting for a series of objections or trying to say the right thing so that person will give you a thumbs up, then you will not necessarily do horribly, but more than likely that client won't remember you after the sale is done, after you got paid.

Over time, you may feel there's not enough hours in the day and there's not enough of you to make everyone a friend or make everyone feel like a family member. I would say to you, "You are right." The reason you are right is because if that is how you feel, and that's how you perceive your time with the people you work with, then that is what you are creating to be your reality. I'm not saying that you have to go out of your way to make every client your best friend, or even someone that ends up going to your wedding; we all know you can never force a relationship.

When I start a new transaction with anyone, whether it's a family member, or a friend, or a referral, or just a name and a number, I am going to treat each one of those examples almost the exact same way. When I say "almost," what I mean by that is obviously if I'm doing a loan for my brother, or my mom, or my best friend, there is no way I could act the same with them verses someone I just met because we do not have history together. But I will say this: for me, personally, it is very hard to pretend to be someone I'm not or to feel like I'm coming across as a fake person. I simply am not good at that because it is very hard for me to learn what a lot of companies out there teach, which are scripts, which are things to say if somebody responds with an objection. It is simply not me and it's just not how I am built. I have worked with a lot of salespeople throughout my career, and I will say, I have seen salespeople close a lot of transactions being someone completely different on the phone compared to how they are in real life. If I'm saying that, then yes, you could get away with being someone you are not and waiting for clients to say specific objections so you can hit them with an uppercut and have the right thing to say. But why would you want to do that? Don't you think your job would be more enjoyable being yourself? I'm not saying don't study people who are already successful, nor am I saying not to know what to say from a frequent objection because that would be not very intelligent. What I am saying is the only way you are going to set yourself up for someone you just met to become more than just another transaction, the only way you are going to have lifelong clients, is by being yourself. The only way to be yourself is to be the same way you would be with everyone else.

Say a person talks about golf, and you do not like golf at all, but yet when that person mentions that they were at a golf tournament, you lie to them and tell them you love golf. That will never be real. That will never make that person want to work with you more nor will it make them trust you more. It may help you to possibly close that transaction, but everything that I talk about as far as keeping customer service alive and going that extra mile by doing what everyone else won't do is never for immediate, short-term satisfaction and always for the long term, the organic growth.

So, you have to ask yourself, would your life be more enjoyable if your clients got to know the real you? I know that sounds like a silly question to most of you out there because you think, *Well, of course.* What I also know is that we have all come across or know someone that goes through life wearing a mask and coming across as not genuine, not real, and I will be honest with you, for me personally it is very challenging to communicate or to even get along with someone who sounds like a robot or someone who comes across as pretending to be someone that they are not. For me, when I want to purchase something or to put myself in a position to possibly acquire more, whether it be buying, let's say, anything from insurance, to going out and purchasing a suit, or even making a bigger purchase such as a vehicle. I want to work with somebody who is real, who is a genuine person. If I sense that person is not listening and is not being real with me, the chances of me purchasing from that person go down dramatically. If I come across someone who is being himself or herself, not necessarily telling me what I want to hear, and if anything, maybe even saying things I disagree with, I know they are truly speaking from the heart, giving me a different way of looking and thinking about things. It doesn't matter if I like or dislike what they say, as it matters more to me that they treat me the same way they would a family member or their best friend. I rather that than a person lie to me, only for me to realize that they lied later on, because when that happens, I will not only not work with that person, but I will never refer them; I might even go out of my way to write something to warn others so that they don't get put in that position. It takes a lot, meaning it's not very often that I write something negative about an individual, as they would have to be exceptionally horrible. If I write or think about writing a bad review on someone or even a company, what I have found is that when I go to write about someone to warn others, there are another 50, or 100, or even more negative comments about that company or individual, which is pretty rare because if someone has enough negative comments, it will be very challenging to stay in that profession, especially in this day and age.

My point is when you are working with someone, like my mom used to always say, "Just be yourself. They're going to love you." The fact is, I will literally tell someone if I'm about to make a purchase and I want to make sure they do the right thing for me, meaning they will do whatever they can to get me the best pricing or the best deal, "Hey, pretend I am your favorite cousin, your best friend, your mom, or your favorite uncle or aunt; pretend I'm your favorite person that you would go out of your way to make sure you can give me the best pricing, the best deal today," You will be amazed by telling someone that how it triggers something inside of them. Most of the time you could tell over the phone that they have a big smile on their face.

The Wow Factor

Also, understand that clients will at times tell you only what you want to hear, but it's up to us as professionals with our experience, laser focus, and listening skills to distinguish whether or not a client is telling the truth or what we want to hear at the time.

Whatever profession you are in, there are always bad, average, and the best of the best. Again. I will ask you a silly question, but really, it's not silly: would you rather someone treat you like family or like a best friend, or tell you everything you want to hear just to make you happy at that very moment? I don't know about you, but if you are like me, I like to work with people who help me to solve a challenge, and I do not want to work with someone nor will I respect them or end up becoming friends with them if they are portraying someone that they are not. Whether I find out now, or in the future, if I sense or feel that that person is not being honest or just telling me everything I want to hear, the chances of me ever referring them or ever working with them again go down 99.9%; in fact, it will never happen. So again to end this chapter, the best way I can put it if you is if you want to have long-term success and you want to give the "Wow Factor" to every single client, then focus on treating that client as if they were your best friend, your mom, your dad, or whoever you consider to be the closest person to you. If you focus on treating them the same way you would treat that person, the odds go up dramatically that you will make a friend who could potentially become like family to you rather than you just closing another transaction and never doing business with that person again

Chapter Assignment
- Are you talking to your clients after the loan?

- What are some of the tools you use to stay in front of them? Remember, in order for them to be clients for life, you have to be in their lives.

CHAPTER 18:

Facing Your Challenges

The only way anyone will grow is by facing challenges head on, rather than ignoring them or pretending that they don't exist. A lot of the material in this book doesn't necessarily pertain to building your clientele list or helping you to sell more to make more money; it's relevant to all areas of your life.

If you want more out of life, you have to be willing to take any challenges you have with open arms; in fact, you really need to welcome challenges, knowing that challenges are ultimately reasons to help you grow for the better—not just by how you overcome the challenges but how you react to the challenges. A lot of us have things happen to us, and we all, of course, have different reactions to things that happen to us—meaning some of us hold it inside; others verbally scream out loud; and some choose to ignore everything altogether and compartmentalize the things they don't want to deal with. I would say there's no real perfect way to handle your challenges. If I were to just say, "Smile and be happy," that would be silly. Only a robot could do that. I only encourage you to handle your challenges in a healthy, productive way.

I now get excited when I have challenges because I know that the bigger the challenge is, the bigger the rewards I overcome the challenge.

I find that dealing with adversity is easier if you are overly prepared. I always say to "triple check" everything, and "it's better to be safe than sorry."

Growing up, I can honestly say that I was taught how *not* to be. It wasn't a bad thing, but I felt like my parents wanted me to have more, to have better, than they did. They were smart enough to know that their thoughts and actions were not what they wanted for their kids.

I truly believe that we all know how to be the best at what we can be. If you think about it, it's really not that hard, but we build roadblocks for ourselves, and we take actions that we know will not help us to grow or to make ourselves better. You will never be perfect, nor will things always go your way; however, if you strive for something that most people would say is out of your reach, then you're going to be giving yourself a better opportunity to come close to your true potential.

A lot of people look at individuals who they perceive to be successful like these people have something they don't. What's funny about that that if you were to ask most of these people how they got to where they are, they would have an amazing story of how hard they had to work, how committed they had to be, and they would also talk about how many times they actually failed. They would even say they had something inside of them that knew they were much more and were capable of greater things in life. None of them would say it was easy and now that they are at the top, they can sit back and relax and smoke a cigar. The thing about wanting to be more or to be what you consider success is you have to work at it just like you would with anything else. The more you work at something, the more challenges you face, which means the more obstacles you can overcome. Success is not something that is a living thing; it does not breathe, nor does it have a body or face. Success is a mindset that you create. You cannot go to the store and purchase success, nor can you ultimately fake success in your own mind. You can have that inner confidence that no matter what challenges come your way, you are going to have a positive outlook, if not make any challenge seem minute. The fact is, nobody can see the future, nor do we have a crystal ball, as we all have a choice, and at the end of the day, whatever you choose will be what you get back. A lot of the most successful people have gone through so much pain or challenges; they got to the point where they looked in the mirror and realized that the only way to overcome these challenges is not only to move forward. Not only that, they realized if they wanted to be a force to be reckoned with, they had to try harder, work harder, and be better at their craft.

The bottom line is if you want more out of life, as most of us do, you're going to have to get uncomfortable; you might even have to crawl through a pile of shit. The fact is, you could find somebody that went through horrific events in their life, and they chose not to let those events define who they are or who they could potentially become.

Success is something that should be treated as if you had to have in order for you to continue breathing, continue to grow, continue to be the person you really are. If your goal is not to be successful but rather to get by, then the fact is you're already doing that. And if you're content and you feel you already are a successful person but want more, then it's because you need to set your goals a lot higher.

If you're somebody who thinks that success is something that you can attain by cutting corners, or you think you can get to a place in your life where you don't have to try nor work at it, then ultimately you're going to have a rude awakening. Success, to me, is the result of everything you do to better yourself, without caring whether or not people see all the good deeds, or all the pain, sweat, or hard work you had to put in to get there.

Success is always getting back on that horse, always making an effort, knowing you aren't perfect and that you're going to make mistakes. Success means not making excuses and turning your back on what society or others deem to be "enough," whether enough means doing the bare minimum or being content with your life and what you have. I'm not saying you shouldn't feel content at times or you should go through life unhappy or ungrateful; I'm saying that the more you do for yourself, the more you try to be better, and the more you do things without wanting or expecting recognition, the more confidence, and therefore success, you will have.

Chapter Assignment

- How should you approach success in order for you to give yourself the best chance?
- What are some of the things you have others say about success good or bad?

CHAPTER 19:

Mind on Success and Success on Your Mind

If you aren't waking up every day and thinking about what you can do to make yourself the person you want to be in the future, then you need to change or alter your mindset.

You either have the right mindset or you don't. Nobody is going to hand you a box with a nice shiny bow on top of it, and once you open it, you will be given success. If you're not obsessed nor are you constantly building your life around being successful—but yet you're just hoping one day that you get success or that you catch a break—then you need to understand not only do you have to go and take it; you have to keep it. And that's not easy.

Along the way you're going to have people who look at you and assume that you think you're better than they are. You may even have people talk bad about you behind your back or even to your face. The good thing is, if you're so confident, if you're so into what you want out of life, you will literally laugh inside at anyone who tries to bring you down. I don't mean laugh in a rude or vindictive way but rather laugh because you're feeling good and know better than to listen to their negativity. You will come to realize their negativity is synonymous with: "Great job. You're on the right track."

There are different personalities out there, and we all know that, of course, success means something different for all of us, but ultimately if you don't consider success mandatory in your life, and you just want to make it through the day, then I have good news: that's exactly what you're going to get. If you're not constantly thinking about how to better yourself and make yourself a better person, whether that be a better father, mother, or better at whatever your profession, then you're working towards the opposite. I believe there is no in between. You either work towards bettering yourself and being the best that you can be, or you work towards getting through life and flying under the radar. Even if you decide you don't need success and just want to live off the earth, make sure you don't put yourself in a situation where you are responsible for someone or something else.

Whether you want to be what you consider successful or you choose to lay low, both options will require you to put in some type of effort. Both require you to have a mindset on what you tell yourself every day in order to keep your situation the same, good or bad. So, if that is the case and they both require you to do something, then why not go all out and put your energy to get what you want? Having a positive or negative mindset is a choice and is not a gift that some people just are born with.

So, what are some things you can think of that you can do today in order to have a positive mindset? When I was growing up, my Dad watched the news every night as well as read the local paper, which he still does every night. I chose not to watch the news nor read the paper, as they only put negative stories on, as that is what sells. I choose not to be a part of that. If it's not going to get me close to my goals, then I'm not doing it.

If you have trouble answering that question and you feel that thinking about success and wanting it too much could be a bad thing, then you really have to sit down and evaluate all the reasons why you want success and evaluate all the things that could happen to you if you don't have success.

For me, success was not something I grew up thinking I had to make a choice about; I thought success was something everyone wanted. As I got older, I started to realize that not everyone thinks this way. When you're a kid, you have things that you want for yourself, but some people let these dreams slip away. These are the people who will try to talk you out of pursuing success. You will also notice people who have not given up on their dreams, and these people will cheer you on, they will encourage you, they will tell you yes, get it all, and never stop. They know what it takes to get there, whether they are what they perceive to be successful or they are in the same boat, working towards their success in whatever area of life they are focused on.

The one thing I would say to anyone who is following or listening to negative advice, is there are a lot of things that society or people tell you are good or bad for you, but you have to use your common sense. I tell my kids this all the time. You will see that most successful people do not follow quote unquote "society's rules."

Let's be honest. There are a lot of things that society will deem acceptable or even good for you. What happens over time, as the trends start to change, is that common sense emerges. Things that are bad for you will eventually start to die out—take smoking, for example.

A large portion of society encourages people, especially young people, to drink alcohol, sometimes to the point of excess. Again, use your common sense. How would someone with a success mindset approach this versus someone who is not focused on success?

Building a mindset around success is a muscle you must develop and maintain. If you choose to treat success as an option or you look at success as something that other people have and you don't, then you are going to find yourself working towards failure.

Chapter Assignment

- Write down any negative thoughts you have about success. Then, right next to these statements, write down a positive replacement thought. Keep this handy, and anytime that negative thought comes up, replace it with your positive thought. If you forget, just keep reminding yourself until it is effortless.

CHAPTER 20:

Sharpening Your Sword

What are you doing to learn more about your profession? A lot of people, not people just in sales but individuals who are plumbers, doctors, attorneys, etc., all have opportunities to give back more to their clients. Yet the average individual only does what is required for them to keep their license and to stay up to date with their profession. That is why there is only a small percentage of individuals who are at the top of their professions; these people ask themselves every day, *What value could I bring to my clients that will continue to not only help them but others?*

Depending upon what profession you are in, there are many things out there that you can utilize to bring more value to your clients.

Stand Out From the Rest

If I am going to somebody to sell me tires, then it's up to that person to not only sell me tires but also to keep me up to date on how often I should change my tires, inform me what the best tires are for my vehicle, tell me how often I should rotate my tires, and advise me on how much should I pay without taking from away the quality of my tires.

I'm sure all of you reading this have gone to change your tires, and the person helping you was able to get you the information you needed before they sent you on your way. However, I'm sure that you're not reading this just so that you can feel competent; you're reading this so that you can stand out from the rest in your field.

Let's go back to the tire shop example. Let's say the person who was helping me, like most others would, told me which tires were the best ones and was very knowledgeable. But they went a step further, too. For example, as I left, they sent me a text message saying: "Thank you for coming. Join our monthly newsletter for updates on when you should service your tires so you can get the most out of your dollars spent." Not only that, the next day, the individual who helped me took the time to call and ask me if I had any questions. After I was able to let him know that I was okay, he thanked me again for coming in, and before he hung up said, "Oh, by the way, if you refer someone to us and they use our services, we'll give you 20% off the next time you come in."

That is just an example, a small example, of how you could do so much more by giving it a little more effort. When the sales professional or person in any other profession does more, whether he is learning more about his product, or reading books on how to communicate in a way that allows him to be a better listener, he provides more value. Yet so many salespeople choose not to go the extra mile because they see it as doing more work and not getting paid for it.

Whenever you're tired, you feel overwhelmed, or just have high anxiety and just want to relax but you know you need to do one more thing, as you already promised the client you would—whether it's calling them, picking up important documents, dropping off something you said you would, or anything else that is important to them—make sure you take a deep breath and do what you said you would. Then, call the client and let them know you did what you said you would and ask if they need anything else. They will know you went that extra mile; you know, that thing, that road less traveled. Whenever I say, "I'm just going to call it a night. I can call the client or do that important thing I had to do tomorrow or later," that is when I perk up, because I know that is my mind telling me to do what others will not. I don't want to be like everyone else, not even remotely close. Money is great, but I know if I keep pushing and grinding, working hard and never looking back, it will provide my family and me more. I will build my confidence by doing what others are not willing to do because it's outside the box. For me, helping families, good people, and anyone who needs my help is reward in itself. I know if I do good, then guess what...good things will happen. And they do.

It doesn't do you any good to follow the advice in this book, have success, then, say, six months later, revert back to the way you did things before and stop learning about your craft or profession. The great thing about your mind is the better questions that you ask yourself, the better answers you will come up with. Start asking yourself every day how you can learn more so you can provide real value to your clients. This will help you not only better communicate with them but also, any time your profession comes up in conversation, your name will pop up in their mind, and they will refer you.

Stop Taking Shortcuts
Everyone at times decides to try and get something done faster by taking a shortcut. But I'm sure we have all experienced what happens when we try and do something faster or do something we know is not being done to the best of our potential... What happens? We end up having to go back and redo it, and ultimately it ends up taking more time. Whenever my mind says to just get it done and worry about how it looks later, I know I need to do it the right way and ultimately replace that thought.

It's a habit, and the more you do it, the easier it gets. I still at times find myself saying, "Just get it done," and what ends up happening is it takes longer in the long run because I have to go back and correct the mistakes I made. Just like right now, as I am typing this book, I know if I am not focused and I try to go fast rather than doing it right, I will have to go back, and it will end up costing me more time. Whether I do a blog, make videos, or write an article, I know from past experiences that if I want to save time, then I need to be laser focused by doing it right the first time and doing whatever I can not to takes shortcuts.

You Can Never Do "Too Much"
The best advice I can give to anyone is the same advice I give to myself: do what they will not do, not for more pay or more recognition, but to get closer to my goals. Never allow yourself or anyone else limit what you feel you can do. Think about that. What you feel inside is only the tip of the iceberg, and you can do much more than you could have ever imagined. How many times have you heard someone say "I never even imagined I could do the things I did." But if that is the case, how did they get to where they were at? By pushing themselves to focus on doing more, and when they felt they did enough and it would look or may be too much, they said, "So what? I want to do more because I can."

Here's an example. My daughter had to answer some questions on why she wanted to be on safety patrol. At this point my two older kids were both in it and had went through the same thing, which is to write down why they were different and why they should be chosen out of 50 or 100 other kids, as every kid wanted to be on safety patrol because you got more freedom. Kids have this natural gift to always want to do more, which is why I always encourage my kids to do more and don't hold them back in any way. So, back to my daughter. I asked her to write all the reasons why she felt she should be picked, and when she was finished, before I read it, I asked her if she felt she wrote everything she could think of. She said the paper only had enough room to write one or two sentences, so she kept her answers short. I thought, *Perfect. Every other kid will be thinking exactly what she is.* I suggested she add another paper. She wrote the rest of her answers down, and when she turned it in, she gave the teacher a folder, which was nice and neat, and combined the papers.

You can never ever go wrong with doing too much, but you can always do too little. I constantly reflect, *If I were somebody who needed my services, what are some things that I would want? What are things that would help me learn more? Not only that, what would be things that would make my profession easier to learn about?*

What Are You Waiting For?

I'm going to ask you a series of questions, and if you answer "yes" to most of these, which you need to be honest with yourself, then you are doing more than most people. Do you have a YouTube channel? If so, are you making videos at least once a month, if not more? Do you have a list of every single person that you know? And not just their name and phone number but also their address, their date of birth, and some of their hobbies? Are you doing mailers every holiday? Are you reaching out to your past clients at least once or twice a quarter? Are you constantly calling the individuals within your database, whether you do business with them or not, on their birthdays? Are you sending out birthday cards? Are you mailing at least 20 thank you cards a week? Do you have a testimonial from every client, good or bad, that you have helped? Do you have video testimonial of your past clients talking about you? Are you on the major social media sites branding yourself? These are just some of the things you could be doing. And if you aren't doing them, I realize this is going to sound overwhelming at first. You must realize that your peers are doing a lot of these things already, and over time, the more you do these things, the more you will be on people's minds who need your services.

Don't be surprised if even if you're doing these things, a past client, friend, or family member works with someone else. Even if you do everything close to perfect, you're going to have some of your past clients or your family and friends work with someone else for whatever reason. But the question I would ask is: Would you want to capture 8 percent of the people that you know along with their family and friends, as you are always going to get referrals, or would you rather capture 10 percent? A lot of you out there should be getting very excited about some of these ideas, and I hope your creative side is starting to come out. There's a lot you can do to bring more value to your clients and ensure they become lifelong clients. If you're wondering where to start, when to start, the answer is yesterday! Stop putting limitations on yourself and overanalyzing everything you should or should not do—when the best time is to read or listen to your books, when you should call your clients or email them, etc. When you spend time ruminating over the best course of action, a competitor is picking up the phone, taking action, and taking your business. Strategize a plan and act NOW!

Chapter Assignment

- Write down what you can do to make yourself more valuable to your clients and how that would separate you from others in your profession.

CHAPTER 21:

Knowing When to Fold Them

A lot of people who are in sales are going to either relate to this chapter, or it will hopefully make them see the light.

Sometimes, even though we are doing the things that we feel are going to bring us success, the person we are working with doesn't seem to value our services. Now I'm not saying that you should walk away from every client who is somewhat rude to you or gives you the impression that they do not respect you or appreciate what you are doing for them; what I'm saying is, listen to your gut.

You have to know, as they say in poker, "when to fold them." With that being said, of course, you have to know when to "hold them." When you are dealing with clients, the biggest mistake I see people in sales make is they start off the relationship with one type of personality, which I would describe it as happy-go-lucky, and if anything goes wrong, they try to close the loan like they are the terminator. By behaving this way, you are not only going to lose the respect of the client, you will ultimately do further damage, such as waste your time and disrupt your life until you ultimately close that sale or loan or walk away from it.

So, the way you could prevent having to walk away from a client who doesn't appreciate your time or services is to put safeguards in place from the beginning and set a certain tone for the relationship. Start by going over some key factors and explaining what it is you're doing and what is going to happen during the sales process. Also explain how your guidance will make the process easier for them and will make it more likely they will get what they want.

You also want to take every comment or objection in the beginning very seriously, as this is one of the most important factors that can impact your job. For example, if you have a client who sounds very happy with everything that you are saying and is continuously saying, "Yes, I agree," but you notice something as small as them taking a long, uncomfortable deep breath every time you mention a specific topic, then you must dissect and unravel what it is exactly that is bothering them or what do they disagree with when you touch on that topic. The key to dissecting and discussing these disagreements, which I cannot emphasize enough, is that you shouldn't necessarily be on the defensive end. You have to take every objection and every uncertainty for what it truly is. The reason being is, you have no idea why that client might be upset or disagree about a particular item or subject within the sales process. It could be something as simple as a misunderstanding, or it could be something they feel that you ultimately miscommunicated, or it could be plain and simple that they are right and you, being a human being, are wrong.

A lot of salespeople do address the situation when they have a gut feeling that the client is not happy with a particular subject, but they take whatever the client says at face value. I feel that this is what separates the amateur from the professional, and it's something that you really have to practice to get good at. If you do not sharpen your sword and get better at dealing with a client's objections, you will ultimately find yourself constantly going up an uphill battle. The way to get really good at handling something the client is not happy about is really by treating the client the same way that you would want to be treated. I would suggest you take the time to write down every single objection that you have ever come across and really put yourself in those clients' shoes. Think about what pain or discomfort you would feel and try to empathize. This exercise is not to determine whether that client is right or wrong because again, it goes back to real-life communication.

It does not matter at all if that client is right or wrong; all that matters is at that moment is how they feel. The first step is to address the discomfort, and the second step is to genuinely sympathize with how they feel, just as you would sympathize with a toddler who started to cry because they didn't get their way. You wouldn't try to figure out what the problem is, then, right off the bat, tell that toddler all of the reasons they are wrong, as that toddler would get more upset. If anything, you would naturally figure out the problem first, then sympathize.

So, after you sympathize, you then want to repeat back what that person's objection based on how you're hearing it. The reason for this is that you are letting them know that you understand what is wrong; you understand how they feel.

Now, the reason I called this chapter "Knowing When to Fold Them" is very simple, and the "fold them" part has to do with what should happen if you cannot come to an agreement. If you cannot overcome that objection and you continue to move forward with that process, you are ultimately going to do yourself more harm than good in the long run, even if you still get the deal. Here's why. Let's say that you decide to continue to move forward, even though you know this client is unhappy with a particular part of the process, but you continue to move forward, and you close that loan. How are you going to get a testimonial from this client? How are you going to keep your name intact? The reality is, you won't. I know this is a very hard thing to swallow, but you have to first set the groundwork from the very beginning, and you must never move forward unless you know that client is happy with the process, and if they are not, you must find out why and do whatever you can to get them back on the train tracks. Not only that; you need to make sure once they are back on board that they are very secure. You could still move forward, and your train can still reach its destination, but if your train is not securely on the tracks, it will eventually crash. The crash could be canceling right before they sign the final paperwork, or canceling right after the loan, or, even worse, writing a negative review about you.

I decided early in my career that I would not work with someone who does not value, respect, and appreciate my services, as that would be unethical for me to do. Think about it. If you are going around saying that you are an ethical person and you just want to do the right thing and you provide the best customer service, but yet you do a loan for somebody who is telling you they don't agree with a particular part of the loan, then you are simply doing it for the commission. Ultimately, if you are reading this book, you are like me where, yes, you want to do well and grow your business, but you also don't want to build an unstable foundation. I have been to many sales seminars, and one seminar stood out to me the most. A woman told a story about a group of workers who built a beautiful pyramid but after 20 years of building the pyramid, it collapsed. Now, once the pyramid collapsed, they found out the reason: even though it was nice and elegant on the outside, when they built the foundation, they ran out of the correct cement. So instead of doing the right thing and waiting to get more, they mixed sand with the cement to bulk it so that they could finish the pyramid. They completed this project with a shortcut mentality. They didn't want to wait for more cement because they wanted instant gratification. This inevitably destroyed the pyramid but also destroyed their names. They should have simply folded and come back to play another hand.

Chapter Assignment

- Write down a time when you knew you should have walked away from a client, but you didn't because you were afraid of losing the deal. Remember, you can never lose a deal if you don't have it. Don't get upset with something you do not have; rather, learn from it and don't let it slow down your momentum.

CHAPTER 22:

Don't Be Afraid to Ask for Help

There is a common misconception that when someone asks for help, they are "less than" or "weak." I'm not sure who came up with these rules. All the great thinkers and successes agree that it never hurts to ask for help. If you are the type of person who says, "I don't need any help. I can do everything on my own," then you either have not experienced enough in life or you are the type to make excuses as to why you are stuck. Nobody was born knowing it all. Even someone who has it all has to prove him or herself and make a name for him or herself. If you go through life not building relationships, not building stronger bonds, then you will never be in the people business.

Regardless of what you do for a living, you have to communicate, which is the same as the word "selling," as to me, selling is communication. Now, in order to get to the next level, even Michael Jordan, who is considered the greatest basketball player of all time, had to humble himself and had to admit that he needed help. If you go back and study or watch interviews of successful people, I can assure you that not one of them ever said, "I never asked for help. I did it all on my own." There is nothing wrong with getting help; in fact, most people will respect you more and they will feel good about helping you because most people can relate. Not only that; they feel good that you went out of your way to either ask them for guidance or training. There are many great companies out there that started out with nothing but they had an idea and they asked for help from investors because they had a dream; they had a goal, and they believed so much in this dream that they were able to transfer their energy to someone else, who then ultimately believed in their dream and decided to help that individual.

In addition to asking for help, if you're in sales, you need to have the mindset, the mentality, of doing whatever you can to be successful, to squeeze all the potential that you have. You need to do this so that one day you can be in a position to give help and guidance to those who have helped you.

You need to rethink your beliefs about asking for help. I, personally, have never had trouble with reaching up and asking for help. The reason I say "reaching up" is because you don't ever want to reach down or reach beside you; you always want to aim higher. You don't want to emulate those who you consider successful. You don't want to try and accomplish everything that they have accomplished. You want to not only accomplish what they have but much, much, much more. If you are committed, and you have the motivation and drive and, in your heart of hearts, believe in yourself, you need to understand that in order to grow as a person, there is nothing wrong with you reaching out your hand and asking for guidance, asking for help.

Chapter Assignment

- Name a time where you wanted to ask for help and decided not to. Remember, always ask, and like my mom said, "The worst thing you can get is a 'no'…then, ask again."

CHAPTER 23:

Lucky to Be Alive

If this isn't something you think about often, then this chapter will be really good for you because you should be thinking about how lucky you are to be alive, and it should cross your mind when you're having a bad day. Like I mentioned before, your odds of being born are one in 400 trillion, which is more unlikely than winning the lottery!

With that being said, we all have to ask ourselves: *What can I do to make sure that I am doing everything in my power to live up to my full potential, knowing I am not perfect?* The reason why I say "knowing I am not perfect" is because I really want anyone who is listening to or reading this book know that everything that I am talking about, I am personally living.

You're going to see that the difference between successful people compared to others is how when they fall, they jump back up. Now, of course, nobody likes to fall; nobody likes it when bad things happen. That's really the goal of learning new things, to ultimately prevent yourself from having to go through anything that is going to hurt you or limit who you are, allowing you to live your life to the fullest.

I would say that if you are someone who is always reaching up, then I'm sure you are also someone who has gone through challenges, just like we all have. Some of those challenges were probably so big that you doubted you could overcome them. But you did overcome them, and you will continue to confront and tackle your challenges.

I'm not one of those guys who walks around chipper 24/7, but I'll tell you this: you will never catch me responding in a negative way when someone goes to ask me, "How was your day?" or "What's the weather like?" It could be sunny; it could be rainy; it could be Katrina outside...I'm always going to let whoever is asking me know that I feel grateful and lucky to be alive.

It doesn't matter how you grew up—whether you were middle class, dirt poor, or Richie Rich—your outlook on life, whether you feel lucky to be alive, will impact the way you live your life.

What's also important is that you understand that just because somebody has a negative outlook doesn't mean you should sink down to their level. Don't use others' negativity as an excuse for your own. Additionally, someone else's negativity or unhappiness is not a reason for you to think you are better than that person. Be humble. Be kind. Be grateful to be alive. There are scary people out there—vindictive people you don't want to cross paths with. You see a lot of these personalities on YouTube. These people believe life is about them and no one else. But there's also the complete opposite. There are people who go out of their way to help others, and typically these people have had tragic things happen to them and have risen above it. These people are grateful to be alive, and, despite what they've been through, they have a positive outlook. It's called resilience.

I certainly don't face every challenge I go through with a smile, but I will tell you this: I may gripe and groan about something, but I'll get over it, and my future actions won't mirror what I felt in that moment.

I'm not saying that you have to walk around whistling every day and being the happy-go-lucky, chipper type; what I am saying is this: If you are not focused every day by being disciplined, then your actions and results will reflect that.

The Wow Factor

Like anything, being grateful, or positive, or even humble is a choice and it's a muscle that you either will use or lose.

When I see someone who is doing really well, I'm always going to genuinely high five that person, or encourage that person, or go out of my way to say, "Good job! Go get 'em!" I personally admire anyone who is trying to better their life. I admire anyone who has a positive attitude.

It's easy to throw your hands up in the air and say, "Fuck it. I'm going to ignore the challenges that I have in my life and I'm just going to live my life and have fun," allowing either alcohol or drugs to mask that pain. Now I say that knowing that I was in that very spot. I was that person, and I didn't like who I was. But, as most of us do, I worked hard to give myself excuses or reasons for why I was the way I was. But, I also couldn't ignore the guilt and the disappointment that it came with. It goes both ways. It's an everyday struggle, and it's hard work to be somebody who gives up at life.

Everyone has a choice, and to say it's easy would not be something you would hear from anyone who did something that was extraordinary or outside the box. Hearing about anyone who struggles with drugs or alcohol is something that hits home, as I had a family member who struggled with drugs for a long time. For me, at that moment, the only thing I could was be there for him and just be positive no matter what.

I want to do whatever I can to speak from the heart but above all be positive because to me that will always be more effective. I'm not saying you should lie to someone at all; I'm saying that when I see someone going through the struggles of any situation, but they want to begin to improve, I am going to make sure to encourage it and above all let them know that the first step is to forget the past and move forward by taking positive actions, as we all have to start from somewhere, and the best time to start is always that moment you realize you are capable of more and you will do whatever it takes to overcome any challenges that come your way.

I want to tell you that everything I am writing in this book I am living, and I know that no matter what happens to me, no matter what challenges I face, I am going to be grateful and thankful that I am here and alive on this planet. I know that there has never been a better time to reach my potential with all the resources now available. And if it means that I have to get knocked down 100 times, then I know that failure is not an option, and you cannot not fail if you do not quit.

Understand that whatever happens, you can go around saying it was inevitable or fate, but know if you were to seriously ask yourself if you are where you are at today because of your actions or because of something else, most of the time you will say it's because of your actions.

The same goes for me, of course, I make mistakes, but I also have learned from positive people around me. For example, my wife is a very positive person and always tells me not to dwell on anything that is in the past. Now if my mind starts to dwell on something, then BOOM, I think about what she says, and I reword my thoughts and repeat only positive thoughts, as I know whatever I think about will lead me to my actions. The first action is to consciously and genuinely say to yourself, "I'm grateful to be alive."

Chapter Assignment
- Write down 20 things you are grateful for and keep your list next to your bed. Read them every morning to help get you started. If you forget to read them, then no

The Wow Factor

problem; just keep doing it until it becomes a habit. You can amend your list as your life changes or when you remember something you left out. By writing these things down, your subconscious mind will begin to change its pattern of how you think, and how you think will determine what you have to give to not only your clients but to your loved ones around you as well.

CHAPTER 24:

Building Your Support System

A lot of successful people will emphasize how important it is to surround yourself with positive thinkers; with people who will bring you up and not bring you down. Now, I think the hardest thing for a lot people out there is to have someone close to them who is negative. It's a difficult choice to keep someone around who infuses your life with negativity. This could be your mom, your dad, or your girlfriend or boyfriend. The people closest to us affect us the most. I've read a lot of books on this very subject, and it seems like the authors who write about this subject tend to be of the mind that it doesn't matter who it is; if a person close to you is negative, you should get this person out of your life.

Now, I don't necessarily share this opinion, and have questioned it, as I hope you question some of the opinions I put forth. I don't necessarily believe in cutting people out of your life because you feel like they are not living a positive life or they express negativity. Here's my perspective. Yes, surround yourself with positive people, but if someone you really love and you really care about is being negative, you don't necessarily need to cut them loose. However, you are probably going to have to have a serious talk with that person. It's almost as if you have to give that person a disclaimer.

Here's an example. I had to give this disclaimer to my dad because he is simply a person who doesn't mind being negative. He doesn't mind saying negative comments. When I realized that I no longer wanted that in my life, I also realized I didn't want him out of my life. So, I decided to have a talk with him about it. I told him that while he did not always have to go around being positive, if he wanted to stay in my life, he would have to put on a more positive face around me. I told him he needed to do what he could to not be negative around me.

Now, it's not that simple. The things that mean the most are not that simple. Did what I say, automatically, with a snap of a finger, turn him into a positive person? No, it did not. I had to have several talks with my dad on the subject, but the first one was the hardest. I would say I had three discussions on the subject before my dad realized I was not going to stop until he put on his positive face.

The funny thing about this is, and you will realize this as you get older, that the roles change. When I was a 12 year old, I had no choice. I could not tell my dad, "Hey, Dad, you need to be positive." But as an adult, anything you say, if you speak from the heart with conviction, if you are sold on what you're saying, is going to hit home with the person who is listening.

The great thing about having a conversation like this rather than cutting someone out of your life is that you will start to notice if that person does want to remain in your life. You will notice if they are going out of their way to try and be positive because they know you're not going to be happy with it. You will likely start to see this person working hard to be positive around you, which, I have noticed, as I have done this with many people, tends to spill over into other areas of their life, and that person ends up being a much happier person.

The funny part is that when you tell a person you need positivity from them, they start to feed off of that. For my dad, positivity was almost like a different type of drug to him. I was no longer supplying him with negativity, so he started to get addicted to the positivity. Not only did I see him being positive around me, but it carried over to being positive and thinking differently in other areas of his life. He will never admit to that, nor will I talk to him about it. Some things are better left unsaid.

The fact is, if you look around and you don't see positive people in your life, you need to make a choice. It's the same thing as making a choice of if you want to be successful or unsuccessful. Do I want to live a happy life, or do I want to live a miserable life?

For me, I made a choice, a decision that was life changing. When I met my wife, I decided that I wanted to be with someone who was going to bring out the good in me, someone who, like myself, wanted to live a positive life, and to them living that life was the same thing as deciding to breathe. She didn't kind of want it; she wasn't unsure. It was a choice where she didn't make any exceptions, and this is exactly what I wanted and needed too. Do you want to live that life or not? Will you make excuses for why you won't live that life, or will you man up and have an eye-of-the-tiger approach?

So, when I met my beautiful wife, did I first want to make sure that she had the same mindset as me? Of course. Did I also put her through a series of tests? Yes, I did, and the truth is, she put me through a series of tests as well.

If you and your partner are working towards the same goal in life, you can influence each other to be the people you want to be. The reverse is true too; you can influence a person to be something they don't want to be. Well, that is what you call toxic. What happens if something is toxic? It won't be around very long.

I am glad I made the choice to surround myself with likeminded people. I am glad I made a choice that I wanted to meet someone who would also not accept anything less.

Someone who was just as beautiful on the inside as she was on the outside. My wife is someone who can weather the storm with positivity, who makes the choice to bring positivity to me. I know that I deserve that, and so does she. Marrying my wife was one of the best decisions I have ever made, and that conscious choice allowed me to put myself in the position to do the things I needed to do to be where I'm at today.

Make a choice right now. Make a choice that you will only surround yourself with positivity because who you surround yourself with can alter your mindset. Make the choice to tell people you care about what you need. Don't allow toxicity into your life. You can't control what others do, but you can control what you do.

Chapter Assignment

- Name three people who you can rely on. Express your goals to each of these people and tell them why you feel they are important in your life.

CHAPTER 25:

Asking the Right Questions

If you ask the wrong questions, then you're likely to get the wrong answers. When I am going through any challenge, I focus on what I ask myself, and if it's not getting me an answer that will help me to succeed, then I keep asking until I have a solution. It that simple, and it can be applied to every area in your life.

The reason I wrote this book is I have noticed that in industries everywhere, companies are treating individuals like another number. I treat every client like he or she is my only client and make sure to let them know I will do everything I can to help them. Not only that; I mean it.

This means doing things that won't get you paid and making sure you don't cut corners. For things to flow smoothly, you must be prepared for the many challenges that arise and create positive outcomes for these challenges.

In order to have things run smoothly, when I tell my clients I am going to email them what them what need, I also let them know I'm going to text as well. Not only that; I will call them to make sure they received my email and verbally go over it again to make sure that they do not have any questions. Rather than having my clients worry about whether or not I received their documents, I always email them back, responding, "Received."

The goal is to do whatever you can to take the leg work off of the client. Most salespeople are trying to use technology as much as possible to free up their time and make it so they are required to talk to a client as little as possible. But they still expect to have a client who loves them.

Angel Medina

The challenge with handing off your clients to your staff or a machine is that, while you may close that loan, your clients will remember your staff more than they remember you. Machines will never replace humans, but they can help you to free up your time to build stronger relationships, which will make you new friends, who will introduce you to their friends, and so on.

If you're in sales right now and you aren't asking yourself the right questions, you will end up getting frustrated. When this happens, your questions don't get better but worse. You have to ask yourself, *How can I give more back to my clients?* That means actually giving back more and not pretending to give. You can give your clients something of value when you take the time to learn about your industry, focusing on what you can do to make the process easier. Always make your clients feel like they are your main priority. It will ensure that they not only use your services then but after and for years to come. Let them know you will also be there for anyone they know. Make every client feel like they are your VIP client.

I tell my clients, and I mean it, that they are VIP to me and they can text, email, or call me anytime. Now keep in mind, you will not win them all, but your odds will be better if you're asking the right questions to get the right answer. These answers should give you the ability to provide more for your clients.

This will not be easy, but what I can tell you is that the rewards over time will be worth it. The feeling of doing right by others, not just to earn a commission but to earn a friend, a lifelong client, will start to make you feel as though you're walking on water.

Just remember that the moment you stop working hard and you start focusing on how to do less for your clients is when the ice will start to melt, and eventually you will fall through the cracks.

What I always ask myself is, *What would I want if I was this client?* Then, if I do not like the answer, I ask myself a more powerful question until my answer hits me like a ton of bricks. Now, if the answer you get does not come, and you get frustrated or you just decide that even though you do not like the answer, you will just hope it works, then you will not be moving forward; that action and decision will make it take longer.

If you are someone who feels the clients should love you because you have helped so many other people, or worse, you feel like they should love you because you've done this for so long, then get real! They could care less. Remember, by keeping your ear close to the ground, instead of hiding behind a computer, you will be more likely to catch a problem before it happens.

I mean, how can you ever know how good you really are in your profession, in your industry, unless you face new challenges you have never faced before with your clients? They will not expect you to be perfect, and the crazy part that I have found is that when big challenges come up, the client may get frustrated at first, but because I was there with them and went through it as well, it actually brought us closer together when I solved the issue than if the loan was perfect. Actually, out of all the years I have been doing sales, I had a loan that I did for a client that was absolutely perfect; I mean, normally it could take up to three to six weeks to close, and I was done in nine days and ready to have the client sign. So, here I am, super excited to have the client sign, and I called him and said, "Hey! Great news! We are done. The notary will be calling you in to sign the final loan documents."

And his reaction blew me away. He then said, "Why did it go so fast?"

To which I replied, "Yes, it happened fast, but the good news is you can move forward and spend more time with your family."

He then said he would need more time and felt a little uneasy because I was able to do it so quickly.

I then thought about what he said and realized that he was acting like that because I did not have time to form a strong bond with him. I'm not saying you want all client interactions to be challenging; what I am saying is face every challenge as if it was your turn up to bat and the bases are loaded, like you have four seconds on the clock and you need one more basket to win the game.

I also learned that if the loan does go so quickly to take advantage of it, to get to know my client more. If you are not interested in your clients' lives, or peoples' lives in general, then one, you would be if you asked better questions; and two, make yourself interested because that is how you will grow and build new friendships and lifelong relationships. I'm sure you have heard this before, but if not, I'll say it here: people are not interested in you unless you show genuine interest in them, what they like, and what they feel, good or bad. You are not a robot, and you cannot be replaced. So, when you are working with the client, do not treat them like another number but treat them as if it was your family or your best friend. Treat them like you would want to be treated, but even better than that.

I feel asking the right questions starts by listening, and that right there could be something that you may need to work on first. Listening you the natural human I feel ability to know when and how to ask. It's not only asking the right questions; it's knowing *how* to ask. I don't believe in being deceptive, but I certainly believe in having manners and sensitivity.

So, if you're talking about something very important to the client, or something tragic that happened to them, you wouldn't do it with a strong, firm, deep tone. Let's say they lost a loved one, and you needed to talk to them about whether or not they had a copy of the death certificate; you would ask in a soft, low voice, in a caring manner. Not because it's a sales tactic but because you are being respectful, and if you don't do it the right way, that person may not want to speak with you again. I know I wouldn't, so always have how you would want to be treated in the back of your mind. That does not require a script. In fact, facing a challenge like this with *real* compassion will be better than any script someone will give you to say.

Think of questions as what you have to be able to guide the client, as if they were lost in a big shopping mall parking lot and could not remember where they parked. You would ask questions that can help them find their car, such as, "Where did you last see your car?" but you would start by saying, "Okay. Let me help." Then, "What do you remember seeing when you first got here?" And so on. So, let me ask you, if you could help more good people, how would that impact your business? Would it be worth it to you to show your knowledge or listen more? What would you do to better yourself? I'm now asking you the right questions to get you moving forward.

Chapter Assignment

- What are some questions you can ask to make sure your clients are being as open and as transparent as possible?

CHAPTER 26:

It's Not Them; It's You

When you help a client and everything goes your way, you're feeling light on your feet, and there is a hop to your step. You feel it's just because you're *that good*. You look in the mirror and you whisper, "Dang! You're good, you!" Now let's look at it from another perspective, and we have all been here, where things are not going your way and if it could go wrong, it does.

Let's say they gave your client the wrong information; they forgot to email out the new set of documents, but you called twice to make sure. You felt you did everything right, you then ask yourself, *Why can't they do their job?!* I have news for you— it's not them; it's you, buddy! Yes, no matter what, it's you, and that is something that I struggled with for a long time. So, take this chapter seriously so you can think like successful people do. If you do not work on how you place blame, you'll never move forward. That may sound harsh, but I say that with all sincerity, as I was once there myself.

You see, there are so many things that you could have done differently, and if you were to go back and think of all the mistakes the people around you made, which led to that situation, it wouldn't matter because you cannot change anyone but you. The best way you can make something that went wrong into a positive, no matter how hard it may be, is to simply ask yourself: *What could I have done differently to ensure this didn't happen? What did I learn from this?*

Now keep in mind, we are all human, and I make mistakes and I have challenges happen to me as well. But again, it's never what happens to you; it's how you respond to any challenges that come your way. And yes, it's easy to say, "Oh well," and get on your tin can and start singing about how nobody knows your struggle. I have been there, and yes, in that moment, it felt horrible. And yes, it is natural to place the blame on others who you feel have not done their part. But that will not cut it; you need all the blame on you. That way you get all the benefit from all the learning lessons, and the more you learn, the stronger you get.

When I came across this idea, I thought, *Hey, does this work, or no? Who is thinking this way? Okay, is that person successful? Yes. Okay, I will follow their lead whether I like it or not.*

If you think blaming others is sometimes valid, that in and of itself is a choice. Your choices dictate who you are and who you will become, so I would rather go with the "better safe than sorry" approach and choose to learn and focus on what I can do better no matter what.

But again, like anything, if you're new to the gym and you go for the big weight, you're going to be disappointed. You need to work on it daily and read and learn from people who are where you want to be.

It comes from the inside out. You grow, you learn, and you become the person you want to be. And you never stop. As you accomplish one goal, you're doing to want more, as success is a habit, not a present that Mommy or Daddy gave to you. It's a choice. It's yes or no. It's never maybe.

It's a state of mind. If you get thrown on the tracks and the hurt train is coming your way, you get up and move forward. If you're knocked back down, you welcome it, as you will learn from it until things bounce off you and can't knock you down.

The Wow Factor

So, remember, as long as we are aware of when we are blaming others that is it bringing us further from our goals, we can learn from our mistakes, ultimately helping us grow.

Chapter Assignment
- Why is it bad to blame others and not yourself when something goes wrong?

CHAPTER 27:

Creating Time

Time is not on your side. There is nothing you can do about it. You cannot pay someone to create more hours on the clock. The fact is, there are 24 hours in a day, and every human being on the planet has the same amount of time. So, knowing that you cannot buy time, how is it that some people are able to do more in a shorter time period? How is it that some people make it seem like they have all the time in the world?

Saying you don't have enough time or feeling like you don't have enough time is easy. It's easy to say, "I'm not going to work out because I have other things to do" or "I'm not going to eat healthy because I'm too busy." It's hard to do the things you need to do. But that is just the thing that separates successful people from others; they are willing to be so hard on themselves that it is almost impossible for others to be hard on them.

Anything that you do that most people do not, meaning something that is positive yet challenging, is going to hold a great amount of value. For example, I like to get to the gym when it opens, which is 5:00 a.m. The reason why I like to get there so early is because it makes me feel good and I'm surrounded by likeminded people who are just as crazy as I am. Now crazy doesn't always have to be a bad thing because, let's face it, we are all a little crazy; there's just different levels. It makes me feel like I'm pushing myself in terms of what I'm capable of.

The only way to make more time for what is important is to do things that will free up your time. So, I know that if I go and work out in the morning, that will free up a lot of my time and will benefit me both mentally and physically. I have an alert set up on my calendar which reads "The Perfect Day." The perfect day starts off with waking up at 3:30 a.m. to get ready to workout. Yes, that's right, 3:30 am. That is the "Wow Factor," doing what others will not. And I'm not telling you to do that; I am just saying this is what I like to do to get me going before everyone else. It keeps me sharp, as it helps me to get up and not rush to get to the gym by 5:00 a.m.

Now, keep in mind, we are not robots. We are humans. I will be the first one to say that I get off track. Should you follow my exact methods and get up at 3:30? Probably not. I didn't start doing it because someone else was; I did it because I know myself and what I need to do. I had to be brutally honest with myself. I knew that if I didn't get up early to work out, my chances of actually going would drop dramatically. I probably wouldn't work out in the evening, and it would disrupt other areas of my life and my day-to-day activities like spending time with my family. If I didn't work out in the morning, I would stay up late, to the point where my wife couldn't sleep at night, either working or playing video games.

You need to create time to do things that you don't want to do so often that those things cease to be challenging to you. I don't want to say the word "habit" because to me saying habit implies that you are going to continue to do it regardless and also that you enjoy it. No, there are so many different factors, where you may enjoy what it is you need to do some days, and you may not enjoy it other days. You may do it for a year, or two years, and then you stop for a month, and then you decide to do it again. It's not about focusing when you don't do the things you need to do but rather, making sure that when you do stop, you break the ice. "Break the ice" is a term I like because it implies that you are just going to go for it and not give yourself time to come up with a plethora of reasons why you should not just go for it. Yes, I just said "plethora."

You will often hear stories of people who went from being in a state in their life where they were going nowhere, and it felt like time was moving very quickly, but in a blink of an eye they made a decision that they no longer were going to continue to do nothing. Being who you know you should be comes down to deciding that you are going to do all the things that you need to do, whether you like it or not. Throughout the day I would say that over time, yes, there are a lot of things that I do that I don't necessarily want to do, but I do them because I know that it's going to free up my time, and it's going to bring me more time to really do the things that I really want to do, which is to spend more time with my family and yes, sometimes to just be lazy. Relaxing and doing absolutely nothing doesn't mean necessarily that you are lazy; it just means that you are not a robot; you are a human being. Anyone who has been on vacation before will tell you that doing absolutely nothing is boring and time feels like it's going by very, very slowly and you start to feel depressed if anything.

So, what are some things that you could do that will free up your time? Well, that's not something that I can't necessarily answer because everyone's lives are different. But I do know that for me, the way that I maximize my time is by using more of it throughout the week and for me getting up early does allow me to have more time to do the things that I need to do, and not only that, I'm so tired when I go to sleep that it puts me into a deeper sleep to where I don't need as much rest. I really feel that after reading about a lot of people and what they do, that it's really based upon on who you are and how your body reacts to certain things. I cannot simply sit here and say that what works for me will work for you. I'm simply saying that when you make excuses by saying you do not have enough time to do the things that you need to do, you will never get you to where you want to be. On the other hand, coming up with reasons to do the things you need to do and coming up with ways that you can free up your time will be much more valuable for you.

I always ask myself, *What could I do to free up more of my time?* A lot of people out there won't do it because they're thinking about the short-term effect rather than the long term. What I mean by that is you may need to invest in something to free up your time, but you're not thinking about how in the long run that's going to bring you more revenue; you're thinking of what you'll be losing.

Again, it goes back to the way you think, and the best advice I can give you is don't try and reinvent the wheel and don't over analyze it or even question it because the more you question it, the more you over analyze it, the more time you will lose. Rather, focus on studying and learning from people who are making it happen, who are successful. Almost all of them will tell you the same formula because the formula of success does not discriminate, does not judge; it is simply the product of a series of acts done on a daily basis that continue to grow, and the more actions you take that positively impact your success, the bigger your results. The more you keep adding, the stronger it gets, and the stronger you get, the harder you are to break. So, the best way to do these things to ensure that others cannot break you and to give yourself more time. It's like my wife says, "Don't dwell on what you didn't do, but focus on what you need to do."

Chapter Assignment
What are some things you can do to create more time?

CHAPTER 28:

Just Be You

In this last chapter I want to talk about really something that my mom told me when I was younger, but I never really took seriously. I'm sure most of you have certain things that were said to you, whether positive or negative, that you keep with you, and I hope you throw away anything that was negative and only keep the positive. So, for me, my mom would always say to just be myself.

Being yourself doesn't mean doing whatever the heck you want to, but rather, being you is really being the best you can be in a positive way. The only way to do that is to continue to grow, by working on the things in this book as well as other things that resonate with you. Working on yourself is like pouring water into a glass; if you keep pouring water into the glass, eventually it's going to overflow; it's going to be everywhere. It will spill over into all areas of your life.

It's just like all the actions you take for your clients. By taking action to make yourself better, you will become the best person you can be in terms of helping them. This is necessary to provide the "Wow Factor"; you have to be on your A game. The only way to give someone your best is to be your best. You cannot fake being the best. You cannot fake being number one or coming in first place or winning. Now don't get me wrong, there are people out there who fake who they are, but they're wasting their time because eventually the truth comes out.

The fact is, if you focus on doing all the things that you know you need to do more on a day-to-day basis, it really gets to a point where you enjoy it more and you don't feel like it's hard work. The opposite is also true. When you neglect the things you want and need to do more of, it makes it harder and makes you have to work harder. A series of acts can build success as well as form a snowball of failure.

So, if you are doing all the things that you need to do and you find yourself being where you want to be in one area of your life but not where you want to be in other areas of your life, I think you're successful but not the best person you can be. If you're successful with, let's say, your health—you work out every day and you eat right—but you are not successful with your relationships or your finances, you could do more for yourself.

Additionally, even if you become successful in all areas of your life, you can't stop doing all the things you did that got you there. You can't fall asleep sitting on your throne because the moment you fall asleep is the moment that somebody will take over your throne. That means that every day, you need to focus on the things you need to work on, you need to learn from as many people as you can, and you need to ask yourself constantly, *What is something I can do to be of value to others so that I can be the best person possible and continue to grow?* Success is not a destination; it's a constant, never-ending journey. Positive acts done on a daily basis will cause your glass to overflow, but the moment you stop doing what you need to do to make yourself grow, the water in your glass will start to evaporate.

Success doesn't necessarily mean just making money or being the most popular person, as success is not a popularity contest. Success is your definition in different areas of your life, and only you know what that is.

What are some of the things that are holding you back right now from you being the best person you can be in life today?

The Wow Factor

What are some things you could do to help yourself be that person? What are you willing to risk? What negative relationships are you willing to repair, draw back, from or end?

It won't help just to write down these responses and think about what you can do; you have to act now. If this is resonating with you now, you are on the right path. The fact is that no book, or words, or promises can ever replace actions. Start replacing your excuses with actions.

The moment you feel like you want to give up, the moment you think to yourself, *I cannot keep doing this*, and you just want to throw your hands into the air, even though you know in your heart of hearts that you are doing the things that you need to do, then that is the moment you push even harder. Remember, you cannot fail if you do not give up. So, just be you.

Thank you again for reading this book in its entirety, and I hope you felt what I put into this book, which is my heart and soul, in hopes that it changes your life so that you can go out and change others people's lives—whether it's in your career or in your relationships.

If you really want to know in summary what the "Wow Factor" is, if you were to really narrow it down, then it's simple. The "Wow Factor" is being the best you can be. I mean, truly, if you work towards being more and living up to your potential, and you are focused on doing much, much more, and you still come up short, then others would still look at you and know you have it— you have the "Wow Factor."

Chapter Assignment
- Describe the best you.

ABOUT THE AUTHOR

Angel Medina was born and raised in San Diego and has been in sales for over 20 years. He utilizes his many years of experience combined with ever-increasing knowledge to consult good people to make the best decisions for themselves and their families. To Angel, selling is helping, and helping equals more valuable relationships, which is better than any commission check.

Angel's passion is to help others by sharing the experiences that have allowed him to continue to do what he loves in hopes that it helps others to do what they love.

Angel is also a doting husband to his beautiful wife, Lana, and proud father of four awesome kids, Cassondra, Logan, Jasmine, and Aubrey, as well as a son, brother, and friend. The people in his life are the reason he wants to provide real value to others and contribute his knowledge and experience. Angel believes we make a living by what we give, not what we make.

Dear Reader,

Thank you for reading *The Wow Factor in Sales: Building Lifelong Relationships*! If you consider this book a to be a valuable asset to your business, career, or personal life, please consider sharing it with a friend, coworker, or family member. My goal is to assist, educate, and bring value to others in their pursuit of long-term happiness and success. Additionally, if you enjoyed this book, please consider leaving a review on Amazon or Goodreads. Every positive review helps me reach more people!

Wishing you a lifetime of success and growth,

Angel David Medina